COMMUNISM NATIONAL AND INTERNATIONAL

COMMUNISM

NATIONAL

AND INTERNATIONAL

Eastern Europe after Stalin

═══

H. GORDON SKILLING

───

Published in association with the
Canadian Institute of International Affairs
by University of Toronto Press

The Canadian Institute of International Affairs is an unofficial and
non-partisan organization founded in 1928 and incorporated in 1950.
As such, it does not express an opinion on any aspect of international
affairs. The views expressed therefore in its publications are those of
the writers and not of the Institute

To David and Peter

PREFACE

THE BUILDING OF THE BERLIN WALL in August, 1961 sealed the one open passage between the communist world in Eastern Europe and the Western countries. Thereafter it became as difficult to move from East to West Berlin as it had been for years to move from Czechoslovakia or Hungary to Austria, or even from one communist country to another. A foreigner could, however, cross these "iron frontiers" with relative ease. During the year "after the wall," I travelled about 10,000 miles in the Eastern European communist countries, crossing and re-crossing the borders by car and by plane. Only Albania remained inaccessible. Constant efforts to secure a visa were of no avail, even after Albania's break with the U.S.S.R. and the establishment of a diplomatic mission in Vienna.[1]

My travels were based on the assumption of the significance of national communism in Eastern Europe, and were intended to assess the impact of the XXII Congress of the Communist party of the Soviet Union on this phenomenon. In the past, the study of communism has tended either to assume its uniformity everywhere, or to concentrate on the description of individual communist states or movements. There has been little or no effort to make a systematic comparative analysis, in particular of the eight countries of Eastern Europe, and to probe more deeply into the causes of the distinctive course of each. My own impressions, as set forth in this book, represent only a rudimentary contribution to the more thorough-going scholarly

[1]See my "Communism in Eastern Europe, Personal Impressions 1961–62," *Canadian Slavonic Papers*, VI, 1964, pp. 18–37.

study so urgently needed. Needless to say, a comparative approach along these lines is fraught with great difficulty and will not provide any quick or easy explanation of the national differences within communism. The multiplicity of languages involved, and the variety of traditions and of local conditions, make the problem one that can be solved only with the aid of specialists on all the countries of this area, and of scholars from many disciplines. The analysis would have to search behind surface appearances and customary *clichés*, and come to grips with the host of factors which have a bearing on the problem—the divergent nature of Communist party leaderships, the distinctive historical evolution of socialism and communism, the diverse manner of the rise of communism to power, the varying impact of Stalinism and de-Stalinization, differing doctrinal interpretations and factional rivalries among communists, as well as the even more profound and complicated contrasts in political tradition, economic evolution, ethnic character, religious patterns, and cultural and intellectual orientation. An article by Robert V. Daniels, "The Chinese Revolution in Russian Perspective,"[2] suggests what still remains to be attempted for Eastern European communism and challenges specialists on this region to make a comparable effort.

Most of the articles which are reproduced without essential change in this book were based on extensive interviewing in the U.S.S.R. and other communist countries during 1961 and 1962, and on prior and subsequent research in Vienna and Toronto. Thanks to a leave from the University of Toronto and grants in aid of research from the Canada Council and the Social Science Research Council, New York City, a year was spent in Vienna, and about half of that time in communist countries. Visits were made to East Germany and Poland in September and October, 1961; to Czechoslovakia, in September, 1961 and April, 1962; to the U.S.S.R., in November and December, 1961; to Hungary, in February and June, 1962; to Bulgaria, in April and July, 1962; to Yugoslavia, in May and July, 1962; and to Rumania, in June, 1962. Interviews were

[2]*World Politics*, XIII, No. 2 (January, 1961), pp. 210–30.

also conducted in London, Bonn, Berlin, Munich, and Vienna. Thanks go to the officials of all the countries visited; to the Canadian, British, and American diplomatic missions; to the Eastern European correspondents of the *New York Times, The Times* of London, and other newspapers; to several hundred other persons in these countries; and to the United States Information Office in Vienna, and Radio Free Europe in Munich for the use of their files and facilities, as well as for translations of materials in Albanian, Bulgarian, Polish, Serbo-Croatian, and Rumanian.

My appreciation is also expressed to Professors James Eayrs and Robert Spencer, editors of the *International Journal,* and to Mr. John Holmes, President of the Canadian Institute of International Affairs, for their encouragement and support in the publication of these articles. I am also indebted to Professor Richard Gregor for his assistance in my translations from Czech and Slovak. I am especially grateful to my wife, Sally, who, with my two sons, David and Peter, sometimes accompanied me on my journeys and sometimes patiently awaited my return to Vienna, and who contributed much by her painstaking editorial work and criticism.

H.G.S.

Toronto,
August, 1964

CONTENTS

CONTENTS

COMMUNISM NATIONAL AND INTERNATIONAL

1

COMMUNISM: NATIONAL OR INTERNATIONAL?*

"TODAY NATIONAL COMMUNISM is a general phenomenon in Communism," writes Milovan Djilas, a former leader of Yugoslav communism. "To varying degrees all Communist movements . . . are gripped by national Communism. . . ."¹ "In essence, Communism is only one thing, but it is realized in different degrees and manners in every country." "No single form of Communism, no matter how similar it is to other forms, exists in any way other than as national Communism. In order to maintain itself, it must become national."²

Whatever the validity of this reasoning, it is hard to deny the fact of national communism. Towards this fact, however, Western thought and policy have been ambivalent, torn between two conflicting impulses: on the one hand, to regard world communism as a single monolithic movement, controlled by Moscow, and on the other hand, to hope for its weakening through some form of national communism, à la Tito, especially in China. During the climactic year 1956, this ambivalence received dramatic expression in the reaction of the West towards events in Poland and Hungary. The resistance of Polish and Hungarian communists (and in the latter case, of non-communists, too) to the Soviet Union was fervently welcomed, but was not aided in any positive manner. Although

*Published in International Journal, XV, No. 1 (Winter, 1960).
¹Milovan Djilas, The New Class (New York, 1957), p. 181.
²Ibid., pp. 173, 174.

there were many causes of Western passivity, an important ingredient was the lack of a strong belief in the reality, or the desirability, of national communism. Similar ambiguities had permeated Western policy towards Yugoslavia in the preceding decade.

Yet, if these crucial events in 1956, as well as the Soviet-Yugoslav break in 1948, demonstrated anything, it was that national communism was a reality and indeed a force ultimately capable, in certain circumstances, of transforming the entire communist world. Our current assumptions concerning communism, however, prevented us from appreciating this fact and offered us little guidance in these past crises. The slogan of "liberation from communism," for instance, was hardly helpful in 1956. A careful assessment of the meaning and the potentialities of national communism might provide us with a basis for a more rational attitude and policy towards the future march of events in Eastern Europe and the communist orbit.

It is well over a century since Marx and Engels, in the *Communist Manifesto*, uttered the stirring words: "Workers of the world, unite!" This appeal, which has never ceased to inspire the communists of the world, may still be found every day under the title of *Pravda*, organ of the Communist party of the Soviet Union. As used by Marx and Engels, these words expressed their profound conviction, as they put it elsewhere in the same document, that "the working men have no country," that "national differences and antagonisms between peoples are daily more and more vanishing," and that "the supremacy of the proletariat will cause them to vanish still faster."[3] Marxism, an international doctrine from the first, assumed that the victory of the workers and the establishment of socialism would eliminate national conflicts and safeguard the peace. Similarly, communism, as an outgrowth of Marxism, still assumes that nationalism and communism are opposites and that in a world of communist rule, nationalism and national

[3]"Manifesto of the Communist Party," *in* Karl Marx, *Selected Works* (New York, no date), I, p. 225.

hostilities, and therefore war, would disappear. Thus the Soviet periodical *Kommunist* once wrote: "The very expression national communism is a logical absurdity. By itself communism is really international and it cannot be conceived otherwise."[4] Even Tito, usually regarded as the apostle of national communism, has declared: "National communism doesn't exist. Yugoslav Communists too are internationalists."[5]

The October Revolution in 1917, however, produced strange consequences in the development of Marxism as an internationalist doctrine. For almost thirty years there was only one communist state in the world. Nationalism had an increasing impact on the Soviet Union under these circumstances. In view of the failure of world revolution, Lenin's attention was more and more centred on Russia and Russian problems. Stalin's doctrine of "socialism in one country," as opposed to Trotsky's "permanent world revolution," reflected these facts and also gave expression to a deeply patriotic note, placing Russia, and not world communism, in the centre of things.[6] By the late twenties even the Communist International had come to have as its main purpose the defence of the Soviet Union, rather than the direction of a world revolution.[7] The Communist parties of the world were so moulded by the Comintern, and by Stalin personally, that their loyalty was pointed towards the Soviet state in Russia rather than to the international working class. As Stalin put it in 1927, "A *revolutionary* is one who is ready to protect, to defend the U.S.S.R. without reservation... for the U.S.S.R. is the first proletarian, revolutionary state in the world. . . ."[8] A communist not so animated with love and devotion for the U.S.S.R. was a "bourgeois nationalist." Thus

[4]Quoted by Bernard Morris, "Soviet Policy Toward National Communism: The Limits of Diversity," *The American Political Science Review*, LIII, No. 1 (March, 1959), p. 128.

[5]*Ibid.*, p. 128.

[6]I. Deutscher, *Stalin: A Political Biography* (New York and London, 1949), pp. 327–8.

[7]M. Florinsky, *World Revolution and the U.S.S.R.* (New York, 1933), p. 208.

[8]Bernard Morris, "Soviet Policy Toward National Communism," p. 130.

by a strange turn of events Marxist internationalism was transformed into a kind of nationalism: loyalty to the one existing communist state—the Soviet Union.

As long as the Soviet Union alone was communist, nationalism within the international communist movement could be handled without too much difficulty through two chief devices. There was, in the first place, the ideological cement of Marxist-Leninist theory and its interpretation by Stalin. The latter, the high priest of orthodoxy, laid down the line of strategy and tactics, in theory and in practice; deviations to right or to left were extirpated; communists everywhere had either to accept the party line or suffer the penalty of expulsion. As for the coming of proletarian revolution and of socialism, the official theory proclaimed a single path to socialism, or as Lenin put it, "the historical inevitability of a repetition on an international scale of what has taken place here" (i.e. in the U.S.S.R.).[9]

In the second place, there was the organized control of foreign Communist parties through the medium of the Communist International. Meetings of the Comintern organs, especially the Executive Committee and its Presidium, served as the means of control, determining policy and nominating leadership for the entire movement. This instrument, under the firm control of the Soviet party and of Stalin personally, was always able to detect and eliminate heresies, throwing its support to those sections and those leaders willing to espouse the party line of the moment. Where necessary, a whole party, such as the Polish, was dissolved; short of this, the elevation of a new leadership, as in the case of Gottwald in the Czechoslovak party in 1929, or Tito, in 1934, in Yugoslavia, contained nationalistic tendencies and preserved international unity.

The situation was fundamentally changed after 1945, with the emergence of new communist states, at first in Eastern Europe, and then in Asia, so that eventually more than a dozen communist states were in existence. At once the phenomenon of "national communism" took on different forms and previous methods of control proved ineffective. The sharpest manifestation of this new trend has been, of course, Yugoslav commu-

[9]Lenin, *Selected Works* (New York, 1935–8), X, p. 57.

nism, since 1948 standing apart from the Soviet bloc and following its own domestic and foreign policies. At the beginning of the breach with Russia, Tito, himself a product of the Comintern and one of its active workers in the thirties, gave classic utterance to his nationalism in the words, "No matter how much each of us loves the land of socialism, the U.S.S.R., he can, in no case, love his country less, which also is developing socialism. . . ."[10] The Cominform, successor to the Comintern as the vehicle of organizational control, showed itself inadequate to deal with the Yugoslav dissent. Equally helpless in this case were new methods of restraint now available to the Soviet Union: military, diplomatic, and economic pressure on the other communist states, and direct influence on the ruling parties through secret police and party channels. In the decade and more since the rupture, Yugoslav communism has become increasingly national in two important aspects: complete independence from Soviet domination, a position vindicated by years of resistance to Soviet pressures; and the development of its own distinctive institutions and procedures, or as the Yugoslavs would put it, their own "path of socialist development."

Two schools of thought had thus crystallized within the world communist movement—the monistic conception pronounced by Stalin and the U.S.S.R., and the pluralistic conception represented at that time only by Tito and Yugoslavia. Stalin's monistic conception was a projection of the traditional pre-war view and continued down to his death in 1953. It is still held by the so-called Stalinists in Russia and elsewhere. According to this standpoint, communism was one and indivisible, a single, monolithic bloc, tightly bound together under Soviet leadership. A single dogmatic ideology—Marxism-Leninism, as interpreted by one authorized interpreter, must prevail. There is one and only one path to socialism—the Soviet path. All countries moving towards socialism must take the course already traversed by Soviet socialism. Revolution elsewhere must follow the Soviet pattern. The sole organ of international communism—the Cominform—would serve as the vehicle of

[10]*The Soviet-Yugoslav Dispute* (London and New York, 1948), p. 19.

policy transmission, and if necessary, of chastisement of dissidence. This monistic view treated all communist states, China
included, in the same way, as integral parts of an organic
whole. Needless to say, ideological and organizational bonds of
solidarity were to be reinforced by others no less potent, if not
so much discussed—military, economic, and political controls
in the hands of the leading country of the bloc. In actual fact,
China enjoyed a unique status, less in accord with the pure
theory of monism, since it was not under direct Soviet military
or even economic, hegemony, and was united with the U.S.S.R.
by ideological harmony and by voluntary association.

The Yugoslav view of communism was pluralistic, seeing
it as "a house of many mansions," each independent of Soviet
mastery, and each having its own design and style. The
ideology of Marxism was common to all, but there could be
variations on the common theme, with no orthodox version
enunciated by Moscow. Each communist state had the right to
develop its own brand of socialism, or communism, according
to its own needs and conditions. There were "many roads to
socialism." There was no need for a rigid, centralized, international organization such as the Cominform. Co-operation
among equals was desirable and could be attained through
institutions of looser voluntary co-ordination. Above all, any
efforts at military or economic subordination and exploitation
of weaker communist states was rejected as an expression of
great power politics inappropriate to a communist world.[11]

The continued existence of Yugoslav communism was a standing challenge to the Soviet concept of communist monism, and
indeed to the very unity and continuance of the bloc. It was a
negation of the essential uniformity of communism as preached
by Moscow. It was an example for other communists within the
bloc. It was a pattern of an alternative resolution of the contradiction of nationalism and communism. It was a model of
"national communism." As long as Stalin lived, the response of
the U.S.S.R. was the conventional one. Only the Soviet Union

[11]A full statement of the Yugoslav view was given in *The Programme
of the League of Yugoslav Communists* (Belgrade, 1958), especially
pp. 46–9, 54–5, 71.

and its loyal satellites were "really" communist. Yugoslav divergence was heretical and not to be tolerated. Any repetition of the Titoist heresy elsewhere would be similarly treated.

The succession of Khrushchev opened up a new phase of world communism, the final implications of which are still uncertain. Shortly after his assumption of power, two shattering events occurred. The first was the visit of the new Soviet leader to Belgrade in February, 1955, his *rapprochement* with Tito, and the issuance of a joint *communiqué* accepting the doctrine of "many roads to socialism," followed shortly thereafter by the dissolution of the Cominform.[12] The second was the denunciation of Stalin in Khrushchev's speech at the XX Congress of the C.P.S.U. in February, 1956, which apart from its impact on Soviet domestic politics, had tremendous repercussions on communism abroad and on the unifying force of Stalinism.[13] These, and subsequent developments, appeared to amount to an acceptance by Khrushchev of Tito's pluralistic conception of world communism. The Yugoslav national path was endorsed, and her right to follow a different route than the Soviet Union was vindicated. The possibility was thus opened up for other communist states to follow suit and enter on many different roads to socialism. Moreover, there was an implicit recognition of the right of all communist states, on the Yugoslav model, to be completely independent of Moscow rule. No doubt it was assumed that the communist states would voluntarily associate themselves with each other and with the U.S.S.R. in what later came to be called "the great commonwealth of socialist nations."[14] Implied, too, was the recognition by these new communist "dominions" that "equality of status" would not necessarily imply "equality of function" and that there would be continued Soviet primacy within the bloc. It was probably hoped that this new form of association would

[12]Paul E. Zinner (ed.), *National Communism and Popular Revolution in Eastern Europe* (New York, 1956), pp. 6, 11.

[13]*The Anti-Stalin Campaign and International Communism* (New York, 1956), contains the secret speech and other documents from world communism.

[14]The phrase used in the declaration by the Soviet government of Oct. 30, 1956, given in Zinner, *National Communism*, p. 485.

win Yugoslavia back to the fold and end the damaging rift within world communism.

This was a daring move by Khrushchev, probably attended by considerable opposition within the C.P.S.U. leadership. Certainly this was one of the charges later made against Molotov and others when they were removed from the inner councils of the party in the process of Khrushchev's emergence as the dominant figure of Soviet communism. His manoeuvre may in part be explained as a move in the struggle for power after Stalin's death. Yet it was equally an effort by Khrushchev to eliminate one of the most disastrous features of Stalinism and to embark on a new course of relations with the other communist states. It is dubious that he was willing to endorse the full implications of such a policy, that is, the utter independence of each communist country, and purely national forms of communism, on the pattern of Yugoslavia. What he had in mind was presumably what he was attempting within the U.S.S.R. itself: a carefully regulated liberalization of communist society, eradicating the worst evils of Stalinism, but preserving the essential features of the original system. Such a process had already been going on in Yugoslavia for five years. Within Russia this was eventually to work well; basic changes have been effected but without any threat to the system as such. Why not attempt a cautious relaxation within the bloc as a whole, granting a degree of autonomy to each member, and in return winning continued loyalty and the recognition of Soviet pre-eminence? Even under Stalin there had been a precedent for such a system of "co-ordinated diversity" during the years 1945 to 1948, when the "people's democracies" in Eastern Europe had, with the consent, and indeed the sponsorship, of the Soviet Union, been encouraged to follow their "national paths" to socialism, a system which had been brought to an abrupt close in 1947 with the establishment of the Cominform and the identification of the "people's democracies" as "dictatorships of the proletariat" following the common Soviet path.[15]

15H. Gordon Skilling, "People's Democracy, the Proletarian Dictatorship and the Czechoslovak Path to Socialism," *The American Slavic and East European Review*, X, No. 2 (April, 1951), pp. 100–106; " 'People's Democracy' in Soviet Theory," *Soviet Studies*, III, Nos. 1 and 2 (July and October, 1951), pp. 16–33, 131–49.

This well-laid scheme was soon to "gang aft agley." The "controlled thaw" became a flood. The shock of the attack on Stalin and Stalinism led many communists outside the Soviet Union to a reappraisal of their basic beliefs and the policies based thereon, sometimes culminating in a final break with the Communist party, and sometimes to attempts at reformulation of the essential meaning of communism. In non-communist countries, even such a veteran Comintern leader as the Italian, Togliatti, severely criticized the mistakes of the Cominform and spoke of a future "polycentric" communism, modelled on Soviet-Yugoslav relations.[16] Howard Fast, in *The Naked God*, explained how the secret speech against Stalin had brought him to the end of the road of communism.

In communist countries, radical changes in policy and leadership were occurring, reaching the extreme in Poland and Hungary, where Stalinism was partially dismantled and a new course entered upon. Things began to get out of hand, however. National communism began to be interpreted as complete equality with the Soviet Union, culminating in Poland in the resistance in October, 1956, of the Polish communists to Soviet demands. Liberal communism proceeded further and further in the direction of complete freedom of art, of speech, and of association, culminating in Hungary in the revolution against Soviet domination.[17] The compromise settlement in Poland, although forced upon the Soviet leadership by Polish resistance, seemed to embody to some degree the conception of communist "dominion status." Ironically, however, the full statement of the doctrine of a socialist commonwealth, referred to earlier, was made between the two interventions of the Soviet army in Hungary. The crushing of the Hungarian revolt seemed to mark the end of the experiment in the creation of a commonwealth of communist nations. Tito, the spokesman of pluralism, bitterly criticizing and yet in the end reluctantly justifying the Soviet intervention, saw hope only in the eradication of Stalinist elements from bloc leadership; he was

[16]*The Anti-Stalin Campaign and International Communism*, pp. 136–9, 215–8.

[17]Documents on developments in Poland and Hungary are given by Zinner, *National Communism*.

answered in *Pravda* by sharp criticism of his arguments and of the entire Yugoslav path to socialism.[18]

Out of this sequence of relaxation, ferment, resistance, and revolt, there finally matured a new version of Marxist orthodoxy and of intercommunist relations which reached its culmination in December, 1957, at the Moscow conference of Communist parties. In some respects the statement issued by the conference seemed to represent a return to Stalinism, and to its monistic conception of communism.[19] The emphasis was laid on the unity and uniformity of the communist bloc: "the processes of the socialist revolution and the building of socialism are governed by a number of basic laws applicable in all countries embarking on a socialist path." Titoism was denounced under the term "revisionism," which involved "exaggeration of the role of these peculiarities (of a given nation) and departure, under the pretext of national peculiarities, from the universal Marxist-Leninist truth regarding socialist revolution and socialist construction." The holding of the conference itself in Moscow, and the acceptance by the other Communist parties of the line advocated by the Soviet party, suggested the restoration of a kind of substitute for the Cominform, a conclusion reinforced by the inauguration of a magazine for the world communist movement, *Problems of Peace and Socialism.*[20]

But this was not quite Stalinism of the old kind. There was an accent, in the statement adopted, on the possibility of differences of policy within the communist bloc. The *communiqué* warned of the danger of "disregard of national peculiarities" and urged on the various parties the necessity to "creatively apply the general laws governing socialist revolution and socialist construction in accordance with the specific conditions in their countries." Here was the familiar counterpoint of unity and diversity, of independence and solidarity, a kind of "pluralistic

[18]Tito's Pula speech on Nov. 11, 1956, and the *Pravda* article on Nov. 23, 1956, are given in Zinner, *National Communism*, pp. 516 ff.

[19]*Pravda*, Nov. 22, 1957. English text given in *Current Digest of the Soviet Press*, IX, No. 47 (Jan. 1, 1958), pp. 5–6.

[20]In Russian, *Problemy mira i sotsializma*, beginning with I, No. 1, September, 1958. An English language edition is published under the title *World Marxist Review*.

monism." Autonomy of action, yes, but within the intimate voluntary solidarity of the bloc; differences of policy, yes, within certain strict bounds of common action; reforms in communism, yes, but only within the framework of the system itself. The limits within which this diversity should operate would be set by Moscow; outside those narrow and arbitrarily movable limits, strict uniformity of policy and of ideology would be required.

The show case of the new pattern was Poland: an example of the voluntary acceptance of these principles. Under Gomułka Polish communism was ready to acknowledge the imperative of bloc unity, to slow down and reverse some of the reforms initiated before and after October, 1956, in return for the enjoyment of some degree of autonomy and some freedom of action at home.[21] Hungary indicated an alternative, to be avoided if possible, but to be adopted if necessary: the enforced acceptance of uniformity and unity. Yugoslavia, which had refused to sign the declaration of December, 1957, represented, from the Russian standpoint, the opposite extreme, to be avoided at all costs—a completely independent and unilateral course. In the other satellites, where there had been no serious overt resistance to Stalinism, the old order could be maintained, with minor reforms to bring the situation somewhat more in line with the new conception. In one way or another, all communist states, with the exception of Yugoslavia, had been brought to accept the new dispensation, and bloc unity and uniformity, under Soviet leadership, restored.

This state of affairs continued more or less unchanged to 1961. Polish communism moved closer and closer to the bloc as a whole, both in its internal and foreign policies. Yugoslavia moved further away, especially after the publication of the new party programme in 1958, with its bold and deliberate effort to bring Marxism up to date and to clarify and justify the distinctiveness of Yugoslav communism. The denunciation of Yugoslavia by the bloc became sharper and sharper, especially

[21]See Gomułka's article in *Pravda*, Nov. 5, 1957, the English text of which is given in the *Current Digest of the Soviet Press*, IX, No. 44 (Dec. 11, 1957), p. 9.

by the Chinese, once regarded as somewhat sympathetic to liberal or national communism. The Chinese communist organ, *Jenmin Jihpao*, bitterly assailed the Yugoslav programme as "revisionism" and "neo-Bernsteinism" because it "openly forsakes the fundamental principles of Marxism-Leninism," and accused the Yugoslav communists of "splitting the international Communist movement and undermining the solidarity of the Socialist countries."[22] The entire communist bloc regained a new unity and discipline, closely resembling the Stalinist solidarity of old. National communism seemed for the time being to have boiled down to a strictly limited degree of diversity of action in home policies, especially pronounced in Poland. Paradoxically, China, the most ardent spokesman of bloc unity and ideological conformity, itself embarked on a most distinctive form of action in the establishment of the communes, and on a highly independent course of foreign policy. Titoism remained as a peculiar form of national communism, rejecting diplomatic and military association with the bloc, and insisting on ideological originality and organizational separateness. Yet in its internal reforms, Yugoslav communism had made less striking modifications of communism than had been made in Poland, and permitted less freedom of thought and discussion than more orthodox Poland.

Such was the confused and contradictory picture of communism in 1960. Within the body of world communism two tendencies were operating, the centrifugal force of national communism, and the centripetal trend of bloc solidarity, reinforced by the power of the Soviet Union. It was impossible to predict which of the two would prevail. The bloc might become *more*, or *less*, united. Perhaps uniformity would triumph, as in Hungary; perhaps separatism would win, as in Yugoslavia. Perhaps, as in Poland, Khrushchev would be able to work out a satisfactory reconciliation of the diverse forces, granting enough autonomy and diversity to satisfy nationalistic aspirations, and retaining enough uniformity and unity to satisfy the needs of bloc solidarity and Soviet primacy. Perhaps a new

[22]Text in *The New York Times*, May 11, 1958.

spirit of greater toleration in Moscow would induce the return of Yugoslavia to an association of all communist states on the basis of equality. Perhaps in the bloc as a whole, a stricter centralism would eliminate even lip-service to the doctrine of "many paths to socialism." Perhaps this, or its opposite, greater relaxation, would give rise to more extreme national communism, leading to conflicts and revolts within the communist orbit, and perhaps to global war. Judging by past experience, least likely of all was the elimination of communism as such; much more probable seemed some variation, as yet unforeseen and unforeseeable, of the theme of communism.

2

THE XXII CONGRESS AND ITS
AFTERMATH *

IN CONTRAST TO the dramatic repercussions in Eastern Europe
of the XX Congress of the C.P.S.U. five years earlier, the
impact of the XXII Congress in 1961 was at first much less
striking. The renewed assault on Stalin, this time open and
unrestrained, did not generate a comparable intellectual ferment or unleash political forces capable of producing a crisis
of the dimensions of 1956. No doubt Khrushchev and the other
Eastern European leaders were anxious to avoid the disastrous
consequences of that year, when the stability, and indeed the
very existence, of communism hung in the balance, at least in
Hungary and Poland. This time, certainly, their efforts carefully to control the direction and tempo of change were more
successful, and the modest thaw did not produce a flood.
Nonetheless there *were* serious consequences, often slow in
manifesting themselves and differing substantially in each
country, but having a long-run potential for modifying profoundly the shape and content of communism in Eastern
Europe.

An entirely unforeseen result of 1956 had been the emergence of China as an influential force in world communism,
challenging the hitherto predominant position of the Soviet
Union. Her extraordinary intervention in the affairs of Eastern
Europe during and after the Hungarian revolt had greatly

*Written in 1963 and published in the *Canadian Journal of Economics
and Political Science*, XXX, No. 3 (August, 1964).

contributed to the stabilizing of the situation but had marked the emergence of a balance of power within the communist system and the beginning of a serious conflict of policy and doctrine between the two great communist states. Although the full effect of this Chinese challenge was at first somewhat obscured from view, it became increasingly clear that it would have an even more profound impact than earlier defiance by smaller states such as Yugoslavia, Poland, and Hungary. At the XXII Congress, only the tip of the iceberg of Sino-Soviet differences protruded in the form of the Chinese protest at Khrushchev's public denunciation of Enver Hoxha and the Albanian leaders. The full measure of the divergence was revealed in subsequent years, reaching a climax in the confrontation of mid-1963 and after. The expulsion of Albania from the inner Soviet bloc was no doubt designed to warn the Chinese, and indirectly, the other East European leaders, of the penalty of resisting Soviet directives. The action did not, however, have serious disintegrating results in Eastern Europe, since the other communist states, including even Yugoslavia, rallied closer to the Soviet Union. Nonetheless, the event, and the mounting controversy with China, marked a further stage in the evolution of a communist system, polycentric in form, and national in substance. National communism, somewhat quiescent after the crushing of the Hungarian revolt, received a new fillip from the XXII Congress, and in particular from the condemnation of Albania and the Sino-Soviet conflict.

National communism may take *one* or *both* of the following closely related forms: (1) some degree of freedom from Soviet control of the individual communist countries;[1] (2) some degree of distinctiveness of their political systems, their policies, and their ideologies. This is not to deny, of course, that

[1]"Control" is taken to mean the ability of the Soviet Union to compel other states to take action desired by it. "Influence" is taken to mean the ability of the Soviet Union to affect the action taken by other states. Broadly speaking, the difference between "control" and "influence" corresponds to the difference between "coercion" and "persuasion." There are five main types of Soviet control or influence: (1) diplomatic; (2) political; (3) military; (4) economic; and (5) ideological, exercised either directly on the individual state or through the medium of the organizations of the Soviet bloc.

these national elements coexist with some degree of continuing Soviet influence or control and with the persistence of certain features common to all communist states. The term "national communism" is a relative concept, its significance varying with the country, the period, and the problem under consideration. In our preoccupation with the fact of the uniformity and dependence of the smaller communist states, we have, however, tended to ignore, or to minimize, the fact of differentiation and independence, so much more pronounced since the Moscow congress in 1961.

I

The expulsion of Albania from the Soviet bloc, one of two spectacular events at the XXII Congress, had a significance which was only later revealed in its full dimensions. The beginning of the rift between the U.S.S.R. and Albania may be traced back to Khrushchev's *rapprochement* with Yugoslavia in 1955 and his attack on Stalin in early 1956, and assumed serious proportions at the Bucharest and Moscow conferences of world communism in 1960. It was in October, 1961, at the XXII Congress, that Khrushchev's brief but savage condemnation of the Albanian leadership publicly bared the full gravity of the controversy to the communist movement and to the world at large. As in all historic events, the issues were many and complicated. No doubt, from the Albanian viewpoint, one of the decisive factors was the traditional fear of outside control, and in particular of Yugoslav influence, and the distrust aroused by the Soviet reconciliation with Yugoslavia. No doubt, too, the Stalinist character of Albanian communism was distasteful to Khrushchev in his campaign of de-Stalinization. Albania's cardinal sin, however, was her involvement in the Sino-Soviet dispute on China's side, and her challenge, implicit and explicit, to the authority of the U.S.S.R. in the world communist camp. On the most sensitive issues of bloc leadership, foreign policy, the strategy of revolution, and even domestic affairs, the Albanians identified themselves with the "leftist" or "dogmatist" position of the Chinese, and repudiated what they considered the "rightist" or "revisionist" view of the Russians.

As a result of her defiance of the U.S.S.R., Albania found

herself, like Yugoslavia in 1948, excommunicated from the community of the faithful, and against her own will, and by the unilateral action of Khrushchev, compelled to tread the path of national communism. She thus joined the category of East European states—no less than four of the eight "satellites" —which had, in the short period of less than two decades since the establishment of communism, frontally challenged the Soviet Union on fundamental issues of policy and doctrine. Albania's "success" was complete, and like Yugoslavia, she achieved a status of full independence which she had neither sought nor expected. In a somewhat different manner, Poland and Hungary, in their turn, had defied Soviet leadership, and with contrasting results. In the case of Poland, a compromise settlement permitted her a considerable margin of autonomy in the conduct of policy at home in return for her voluntary acceptance of the Soviet position in world affairs and bloc relations. In Hungary, the effort to stake out an independent course failed, and a new leadership was imposed by force of arms, leaving only a limited room for manoeuvre in a common effort to avoid a repetition of the 1956 catastrophe.

Throughout the following years the chasm between Albania and the Soviet Union remained wide and apparently unbridgeable. From the outset the U.S.S.R. terminated all commercial relations with Albania, and going even further than in the Yugoslav case in 1948, withdrew her entire diplomatic representation from Tirana. After June, 1962, Albanian delegates were not invited to attend meetings of the Warsaw military alliance or of Comecon* and its committees, so that to all intents and purposes Albania had been expelled from the inner Soviet bloc. Both sides professed a willingness to engage in bilateral discussions, but only on conditions unacceptable to the other side.[2] Except for an occasional lull, mutual recrimination on matters of ideology and policy persisted. The Albanians centred their attacks on Khrushchev personally, as the chief architect of an anti-Albanian policy and as a traitor to Marxism-Leninism.

*Council for Economic Mutual Assistance.
[2]For this and the following, see the speech by Hoxha on May 30, 1962, and *Zeri i Populitt*, June 30, Sept. 19, 20, 30, 1962, and Feb. 7, March 27, April 18, June 23, 25, 1963.

The *rapprochement* between the U.S.S.R. and Yugoslavia, from the late spring of 1962, was denounced as a "process of fusion" of Khrushchev's and Tito's "revisionism." Like the Chinese, the Albanians bitterly attacked American imperialism and decried Khrushchev's efforts to reach agreements with the U.S.A. through negotiations, including the treaty on nuclear tests. As the gap between the Soviet Union and China widened, the Albanians and Chinese gave each other mutual support on all the major issues in dispute.

Albania found no support for her position among her fellow communist states of Eastern Europe. Even in those countries which had shared a common experience at the hands of the Soviet Union, namely Yugoslavia, Hungary, and Poland, communists, while sometimes admitting privately that Khrushchev had used methods hardly distinguishable from those of Stalin in 1948, treated this as a regrettable but necessary means of seeking to force Albania to toe the line. No one joined in the attack against the Albanians more vigorously than the Hungarian, Kádár, who in an article in *Pravda* called them Trotskyist in their outlook. The Hoxha régime represented for him the threat from the Stalinist or dogmatist wing of world communism which he was seeking to destroy in Hungary. In particular, he resented the Albanian view of the Hungarian crisis of 1956 and their effort to shift the blame for it from Rákosi's Stalinist policy to the more liberal course initiated by the XX Congress.[3] Not surprisingly, the more subservient satellite leaders in East Germany, Czechoslovakia, Rumania, and Bulgaria, who had shown no will to resist the Soviet Union in 1956 or at any other time, were at one with the others in condemning Albania and in supporting the Soviet Union. Whatever understanding they might have felt for Albania's reluctance to de-Stalinize, communists in these countries evinced no sympathy for its "leftist" course, and still less for its determination to resist Soviet pressure. There were no more vociferous supporters of Khrushchev's line than Novotný, in Czechoslovakia, or Zhivkov, in Bulgaria, the latter manifesting

---

[3]Dec. 26, 1961. Cf. *Népszabadság*, Jan. 20, which wrote: "The Hungarian counter-revolution is a warning example showing where international dogmatism could lead. . . ."

his devotion by paying an official visit to Belgrade in January, 1963.[4] Rumania, although less clamorous in denouncing Albania and China, developed intimate economic relations with Yugoslavia, with the joint launching of the Iron Gate power project on the Danube. Even East Germany, which, because of unfinished business in East Berlin, might have been tempted by the radical views of Tirana and Peking, felt compelled to adopt the more moderate tactics of Moscow on Berlin and other international issues.

All seven communist countries of Eastern Europe, whether Stalinist or anti-Stalinist in their own internal course, whether independent or subservient in relation to the U.S.S.R., thus found themselves brought together by their common allegiance to the Soviet Union, and their support of Khrushchev's "rightist" position. Any individual sympathizers that Albania might have had within some parties such as the East German, Hungarian, or Bulgarian, were submerged by the campaign of denunciation launched by the leaders. All seven parties severed their associations with the Albanian Workers' party, and treated it as an outcaste from the world communist movement. Unlike the Soviet Union, however, the governments maintained slender diplomatic links, withdrawing only their ambassadors, and all renewed their trade treaties with Albania.

The XXII Congress had at first little noticeable impact on Yugoslavia's position. The general tenor of its proceedings was welcomed in Belgrade, but the persistent criticism of Yugoslav socialism and her alleged revisionism was deplored. No secret was made of the doctrinal differences between the Yugoslav party and the Soviet, and especially of their view of the undesirability of a single centre for world communism and the possibility of the construction of socialism outside the Soviet bloc.[5] As the Sino-Soviet conflict intensified, signs of change appeared, beginning with the visit to Yugoslavia in the spring

[4]Later, both Kádár and Gheorghiu-Dej paid similar visits.

[5]Full comment on the Congress was delayed until the publication in February, 1962, of the December, 1961 issue of *Socijalizam*, containing extended comments by Najda Pašić and Bogdan Petrović. See the long article on polycentrism by Puniša Perović, "On problems of Leadership and International Relations in the International Workers' Movement," *Nasa Stvarnost*, March, 1962.

of 1962 of Foreign Minister Gromyko, followed by that of the Soviet President, Brezhnev, and culminating in Tito's triumphal return to the U.S.S.R. at the end of the year. Tito's trip was parallelled, it should be noted, by the simultaneous Asian tour of Kardelj and succeeded the participation of Yugoslavia in the Cairo conference of developing countries. President Tito, after his return, declared that Yugoslavia "could not change its foreign policy," and that the "closest co-operation with socialist countries" did not "encroach on our independent policy" or involve the abandonment of friendship with all, including Western, countries.[6]

Was this the end of the policy of non-alignment, and the return of Yugoslavia to the Soviet bloc? Non-alignment had not in the past excluded support of the Soviet goal of "peaceful coexistence" and of the major foreign policy objectives designed to achieve that end. The decisive factor in the shift of attitude towards Moscow was the deepening controversy between China and the Soviet Union, and the Yugoslav belief that the main danger in international communism, and in world affairs generally, was "the Genghis Khan policy" of China, as Tito termed it.[7] Consequently, in spite of divergences in doctrine and in domestic policy, it was deemed to be in the interest of Yugoslavia to develop more and more friendly relations with the Soviet Union and its allies, and to support them in their struggle against Chinese "dogmatism." In a speech to the Central Committee, on May 18, 1963, Tito, referring to the "international revolutionary working class movement," even went so far as to say: "We must be aware that we are a part of that movement and not something outside it." Even this statement, and the presence of a Yugoslav delegate at the congress of the S.E.D.* in Berlin at the end of 1962, did not indicate the return of Yugloslavia to the Soviet bloc. She remained outside both the Warsaw alliance and Comecon, and was not committed to obey the leading member, the U.S.S.R., still less to take military or economic actions resulting from bloc

---

[6]Speeches given in *Borba*, Dec. 23 and 30, 1962, and the report of the second speech in *Pravda*, Jan. 3, 1963.

[7]*Borba*, Jan. 24, 1963.

*Socialist Unity Party of Germany.

decisions, except by her own free choice. The return visit of Khrushchev in the fall of 1963, while contributing to the more friendly relationship, did not seem to lead to any profound change in the situation.

The events described have profoundly affected the nature of the Soviet "commonwealth" and the role of its members. Although the Albanians and Chinese had been proponents of a unified bloc and the necessity of a single centre of leadership, their own actions had done much to undermine these features and to bring about the very system of polycentrism which both had deplored. The views of Yugoslavia were thus vindicated, although paradoxically she was not willing to apply her doctrine of polycentrism to the Chinese and to recognize the right of powerful China to share the direction of world communism. The immediate result of the Sino-Soviet split and the Albanian defection was to bring the European members of the bloc even closer to the Soviet Union and led them once again to emphasize the idea of a single leading centre. Although a total break between Peking and Moscow might strengthen these centripetal forces, the ultimate effect of these events seemed more likely to stimulate the centrifugal forces and promote the freedom of action of the individual members. This was demonstrated in striking fashion by a country long regarded as totally servile to Soviet will and lacking all the prerequisites of an independent policy, namely Rumania. During the past two years she has resisted full integration in the international division of labour proclaimed by Khrushchev and implemented by Comecon and its organs, and has shown a determination to maintain her own programme of full and rounded industrial development, based on an independent evaluation of her national interest.*

In terms of national communism, as expressed in degree of freedom from Soviet control or influence, we may then classify the communist states of Eastern Europe as follows:

A. *Independent states, entirely free from Soviet control*: Yugoslavia and Albania. Neither is a member of the Soviet camp, and neither is therefore subject to the diplomatic, political, military, or economic controls exercised through the

*See Epilogue for further treatment.

camp's organizational system. Each has exercised her right to formulate her own fully independent foreign policy and to interpret Marxist-Leninist doctrine in her own manner. Neither can be forced, against her will, to obey the commands of Moscow in her external or internal affairs. Both may, however, be subject to Soviet influences resulting from certain ideological sympathies, or from diplomatic consensus, or from the threat of military action or economic pressure. Except for the first factor, such influence of the U.S.S.R. differs not so much in kind, as in degree and in form, from that which it exerts on other nearby states such as Finland or Austria, or indeed from that which any large power exerts on a smaller neighbour.

B. *Semi-independent states, not entirely free of control, and subject to substantial Soviet influence, but exercising considerable autonomy of action in domestic affairs*: at present, only Poland. Membership in the camp, and its organizations, and the presence of Soviet troops, limit freedom of action, but, as her experience in 1956 shows, are not guarantees of absolute control. The most important source of autonomy lies in the nature of leadership, which owes its existence and much of its domestic support to its resistance to Soviet pressure in 1956, is not subservient to the C.P.S.U. and displays a marked independence of spirit. The leaders, however, feel much sympathy for the policies of the Khrushchev régime and recognize the necessity of associating closely with the U.S.S.R. and of accepting its direction. To this extent Soviet influence is voluntarily accepted, and an entirely independent role is not demanded. Autonomy permits marked divergences in domestic policy, and some degree of ideological independence, sometimes going beyond the limit of what the Soviet Union regards as desirable.

C. *Dependent states, subject to a high degree of Soviet control and influence, and exercising a much lesser degree of autonomy*: Bulgaria, Czechoslovakia, East Germany, Hungary, and Rumania. All are subject to control through the Warsaw military alliance, bloc economic co-ordination, and strict ideological and political conformity. Although only East Germany and Hungary are under direct military restraint through the

presence of Soviet troops on their territory, the others are open
to the possibility of military action from Soviet forces in adjacent countries. In none of these respects is their position
different in kind to that of Poland. The decisive factor, explaining their status of dependence, is the submissive character
of their leaderships. Each owes its position initially to Soviet
intervention, and regards the closest solidarity with the bloc
and acceptance of Soviet primacy as essential guarantees of
the maintenance of its régime. Nonetheless, all possess a certain
autonomy of action, manifesting itself, in all except Hungary
and to some extent Bulgaria, in a reluctance to introduce
serious changes in the Stalinist system; in Hungary, in a somewhat freer and more flexible course of domestic policy; and in
Rumania, in sturdy resistance to the economic integration
pressed by the Soviet Union.

It should be noted that the lines between these several
categories are not always sharp, nor are they rigid and un-
changing, as countries may shift from one to another group.
Even where Soviet control persists in the fullest degree, it is
not absolute in all situations, and as the Albanian case shows,
may amount to no more than an "influence" that can, if desired,
be rejected. Soviet power is also subject to some limitations
resulting from actual or potential lack of sympathy with
Khrushchev's policies at home and abroad on the part of certain satellite leaders, or of certain factions in Poland, Hungary,
and Bulgaria, who, although traditionally favourable to a more
compliant attitude towards the U.S.S.R., are paradoxically not
favourably inclined towards certain present Soviet policies. As
we have seen, the balancing of China and the Soviet Union
within the bloc, and the influence of Yugoslavia, exerted from
outside, give all members, no matter how dependent and
weak, some leeway for freedom of action.

II

The other salient feature of the XXII Congress was the
broadening and deepening of the campaign against Stalin and
his legacy of ideas and practices. As in 1956, this assault on

Stalinism was closely connected with Soviet domestic affairs, and represented an effort to discredit traditions and persons standing in the way of the measures favoured by Khrushchev in his refashioning of Soviet society. It was also a useful instrument for tarnishing the reputation of the Chinese and the Albanians by linking them with the bane of Stalinism. As for the other Eastern European states, Khrushchev was no doubt anxious to see them press ahead with a gradual revision of continuing Stalinist features, not merely in symbolic terms, through the removal of statues and the changes of street names, but also in real terms, in the lessening of terror, the broadening of freedom, and a more rational economic policy, all within carefully defined limits which would exclude the danger of a qualitative transformation of the system as a whole. Above all, certain shifts in leadership were desirable, both to exclude from office, or to bar from a return to power, those continuing to think in Stalinist terms or resisting the policies sponsored by Khrushchev and his supporters. Nonetheless, Khrushchev was ready to tolerate considerable diversity of action, including the maintenance of much of the Stalinist legacy intact in East Germany, Czechoslovakia, and Rumania, provided these states acknowledged, as they did, Soviet leadership on the major issues of foreign policy, and, in particular, threw their support to Moscow in its battle with Peking.

In view of the explosive implications of the assault on Stalinism, and the inflammable nature of the materials at hand, it is remarkable how slight were the changes in the social and political order in the year following the XXII Congress. In the states sometimes referred to as "orthodox," in a Stalinist sense, namely Albania, East Germany, Czechoslovakia, Rumania, and Bulgaria, the process of de-Stalinization had been minimal ever since the death of Stalin. Even the events of 1956 left them largely unscathed. Only in Bulgaria were there significant changes in leadership, with the elimination of Chervenkov from the main seat of power, but this was not accompanied by far-reaching alteration of institutions or policies. In the same way, after the XXII Congress, again apart from Bulgaria, the *status quo* was in large part maintained. At the other extreme, in the states normally thought of as "unorthodox," namely, Yugoslavia, Poland, and to a lesser extent, Hungary, modifications in the wake of the XXII Congress were also minor, and the *status quo* was maintained, although for the opposite reasons. In these countries, the worst features of Stalinism had been destroyed earlier, in the years after 1950 in the case of Yugoslavia, in 1955 and 1956 in Poland and Hungary, and again more recently in Hungary. For all of them, the XXII Congress represented a vindication of the line already being pursued, and a safe-guarding of its continuance.

The Congress had its least impact in Albania, East Germany, and Rumania. In Albania, there was no effort to replace any of the basic features of the Stalinist system, and the personal rule of Hoxha, absolute leader from the founding of the régime, continued unaltered. As the dispute with the Soviet Union deepened, the defence of Stalin became increasingly passionate, reaching a climax on the anniversary of his death in March, 1963. In East Germany and Rumania, de-Stalinization was limited almost entirely to the symbolic removal of statues and changes in place names, and to furious denunciations of deviationists already purged, who were made to bear the main responsibility for the crimes of the Stalinist period. Both régimes prided themselves on the absence of the worst aspects of Stalinism in the past and on the consequent lack of need for extensive rectification. In neither country was there any serious turn in policy, only minor alterations were made in institutions and practices, and there were no shifts in the leading cadres of party and state. Walter Ulbricht and Gheorghiu-Dej, who had each held the highest party post during the entire period, were able to absolve themselves of guilt and were the subject of campaigns of fulsome praise.

Somewhat more dramatic were the effects in Bulgaria, although the main outlines of the system remained unaffected and action was largely confined to shifts in leadership. The immediate result was a renewed assault on the former leader, Chervenkov, who had since 1956 been gradually demoted from one position of authority to another, and was now removed from the Politburo and all public posts. His prestige apparently remained great, and Stalinist ways of thinking persisted, as was revealed a year later, at the party congress in November, 1962. Chervenkov was finally expelled from the party, and Traicho Kostov and others who had suffered during the Stalinist period were fully rehabilitated. A new attack on so-called Stalinists was made, this time in the persons of Anton Yugov, Prime Minister since 1956, Georgi Tsankov, Deputy Prime Minister, both of whom were Politburo members, and other lesser figures. The charges were many and varied, including involvement in the worst crimes of Stalinism, resistance to de-Stalinization, and Yugov's ambition to replace Zhivkov as party leader. The fact that he, as well as Tsankov and others purged, had been at the head of the Ministry of the Interior from 1944 to 1962, and were accused of illegalities committed during the Stalinist days, suggested that this major purge was indeed linked with de-Stalinization. However, Georgi Dimitrov, as well as Zhivkov himself, were absolved of all responsibility for events occurring when they held positions of great power, which suggested that the purge was also being used by Zhivkov as a weapon in his struggle against his rivals. Although there was no serious evidence of sympathy by Yugov, or even Chervenkov, for the Albanians and the Chinese, it was not unreasonable to suppose that they were looking to Peking as a balance against Moscow, and as tactical allies against Khrushchev's revisionism. The events in Bulgaria were warmly greeted in Belgrade, in spite of continuing Bulgarian criticism of Yugoslav revisionism, and regarded as a hopeful sign of a progressive evolution.[8]

The initial reaction to the XXII Congress in Czechoslovakia was not unlike that in Rumania, with an assault on Stalinism that was largely verbal, and the assignment of responsibility for past evils to Slánský, executed in 1952, and to a limited extent to the dead leader, Gottwald himself. Even the symbolic measures announced in November, 1961, such as the destruc-

---

[8]*Borba* commented on these events as "a new struggle for an important reorientation of Bulgaria's internal life," but one that will not be painless or quick. "The roots of the old cannot be extirpated overnight. There will be resistance and it is reckoned with. There are no illusions" (Nov. 13, 1962).

tion of the Stalin statue on the Letná height, and the transfer of the embalmed body of Gottwald from the Žižkov mausoleum, were carried out only after great delay, almost a year later, and the changing of street and place names, and the removal of lesser monuments, proceeded at a snail's pace. Even more significant was the slowness of the rehabilitation of those who had suffered at the hands of the terror, many of whom had been released from prison, but without formal revision of their sentences or public exoneration. The report of the commission charged with the re-examination of the trials of the Stalin period was never published, and its chairman, Rudolf Barák, Minister of the Interior after 1952, was arrested and imprisoned on charges of embezzlement in early 1962. It was impossible to tell whether the question of rehabilitation was involved, and whether Barák had stood for more vigorous de-Stalinization, as some assumed, and had had political aspirations to overthrow Novotný, as the latter insinuated. Certainly the elimination from the Presidium of a man of relative youth and intelligence, not so closely associated with the worst of the Stalinist period as his colleagues, removed the only serious alternative leader capable of carrying through a somewhat more liberal programme.

Events which one Slovak writer called "revolutionary" came in April and May of the next year, with the dismissal from the party Presidium of two Gottwald veterans, Karol Bacílek, Slovak party chief, and Bruno Köhler, secretariat member, coupled with an announcement that the rehabilitation committee had turned its report over to the Supreme Court and the General Prosecutor for action. Although this was published only months later, it soon became known that the trials of the fifties had been completely repudiated, and many of the leading victims, including Slánský and his closest associates, and Slovak leaders, such as V. Clementis, Laco Novomeský, and others had been at least legally rehabilitated.

These events opened up the flood-gates of wrath and censure at conferences of Slovak writers, Slovak journalists, and Czechoslovak writers in April and May, 1963.[9] Frank and bitter speeches denounced the crimes of the Stalin period, and

[9]See Chapter 7 for fuller treatment.

openly lamented the failure to take meaningful corrective measures after the XX Congress in 1956. The wave of criticism reached up, not only to the dead in the persons of Kopecký and Bašťovánský, but even to the living, such as Ladislav Stoll, for many years cultural dictator, and Viliam Siroký, then Prime Minister. There were voices declaring that "the fight between new and old" had just begun, that much had to be done to make up for the time lost since 1956, and that there was grave danger of a relapse. Whether the writers had entered, as Novotný put it in a speech on June 12, "on a dangerous road," or whether the Czechoslovak régime, and the Novotný leadership itself, would be shaken by the further course of events, could not be foreseen. It was clear that the de-Stalinization proclaimed so often was beginning to bear unexpected fruit in Czechoslovakia.

Nowhere in Eastern Europe was the XXII Congress welcomed with greater enthusiasm than in Poland, where it was regarded as a continuance of the process of eliminating Stalinism inaugurated by the XX Congress and as a victory over reactionary forces in the Soviet party. The party's theoretical journal, *Nowe Drogi*, described the cult of personality as a system of rule that had "warped and distorted almost all fields of life" and had "done incalculable harm," affecting "everyday human relations and the relations between the public and authority, and the methods of administering the economy," causing "the bureaucratization of social life and above all of party life," and "hampering the development of creative Marxist thought." "The breaking of these fetters became an historic necessity."[10]

Paradoxically, the Congress produced few spectacular results in Poland itself. It was treated as a corroboration of the line which had been followed since 1956, strengthening the hand of Gomułka and requiring no significant changes of leadership or policy. There was no departure from two of the great gains of 1956, namely the end of collectivization, and the *modus vivendi* with the Church. In agriculture, indeed, the proportion of collectives dwindled substantially, and although complete collectivization was still proclaimed as the ultimate goal, there

[10]December, 1961.

was no sign of an impending drive to achieve it by other than voluntary means. Relations with the Church were marred by mutual attacks and new restrictions on its activities, but no fundamental change in its position occurred. Nor, on the other hand, were there basic alterations in the system of rule, with the smaller parties continuing to play a minor role and the supremacy of the Polish United Workers' party remaining undiminished. A spirited debate on the meaning of freedom in science and scholarship during the winter of 1961–62 suggested the high value put upon liberty of thought by Polish intellectuals, but did not fundamentally alter the actual situation. Although Poland continued to be intellectually the freest country in the communist world, there was no broadening of this freedom, as some might have wished, and indeed a certain narrowing of the limits of free discussion was observable. This became particularly noticeable a year later, at the Central Committee meeting in July, 1963, when Gomułka and others waged a vigorous campaign against ideological weaknesses and called for a return to orthodoxy.

The reaction of Hungary was somewhat similar, although with its own peculiar nuances. The party resolution of November 17, 1961, asserted categorically that, having liquidated the cult of personality, we must now "finally liquidate the consequences of old errors and not permit their repetition"; more precisely, in a passage omitted in the account in *Pravda*, these were defined as "self-conceit, conservative thinking, spiritual indolence, thirst for power, and the suppression of criticism."[11] As a result of the Congress, Kádár was in a stronger position to implement his "centrist" or middle-of-the-road policy of cautious reform, in particular his attempt to win over nonparty persons to participation in public life under the slogan, "He who is not against us is with us."[12] In contrast to Poland, the post-Congress course involved a prudent extension of a freedom which was more restricted than the Polish, and which was hindered by much greater Stalinist vestiges. Although the struggle on two fronts was maintained in words, the sharp edge of official policy was more and more turned against the

[11]*Népszabadság*, Nov. 19, 1961, and *Pravda*, Nov. 21, 1961.
[12]*Ibid.*, Dec. 10, 1961.

so-called "dogmatists" and their resistance to the Kádár line. Action was at first taken on the local and intermediary levels, but later extended to the topmost level, with the removal of Istvan Friss from high posts in December, 1961, the expulsion of Imre Dogei and Ivan Altmare from the party in March, 1962, and finally, the exclusion of Karoly Kiss from the Politburo, and of the former leaders, Rákosi and Gerö, from the party, in August, 1962. This was accompanied by a purge of members of the judiciary who had been connected with the Stalinist terror, and the rehabilitation of many punished at that time, and was followed in March, 1963 by a widespread amnesty liberating many victims of the post-1956 terror. Just prior to the eighth party congress in November, 1962, the former Social Democrat, Marosan, for reasons that were left unclear, was also removed from the party Politburo, the secretariat, and the control committee. The congress itself was a quiet one, as far as domestic affairs were concerned, and left little doubt of the stability of Kádár's régime, or its anti-Stalinist course. No doubt there were those in Hungary who had hoped that the implications of the XXII Congress would be drawn more fully and that the attack on Stalinism and dogmatism would provide the occasion for an even more thorough revision of the Hungarian system. From the outset Kádár dispelled all illusions that his course marked the beginning of "liberalization" or that it would, for instance, involve the rehabilitation of those who had pulled down the Stalin statue in Budapest in 1956.[13] He wished to broaden the public support for his régime, but it was to remain a system of rule by one party, itself disciplined and monolithic, which would follow a line of Marxist-Leninist orthodoxy in essential matters, and would make no concessions to bourgeois ideas of freedom and liberty.[14]

Few states had done more than Yugoslavia in revising, long before the XXII Congress, the ideas and institutions inherited from its Stalinist past. Agriculture had been largely de-collec-

---

[13]His speech at the Csepel factory, in *Népszabadság*, Dec. 3, 1961.
[14]See the articles by I. Szirmai, *ibid.*, March 10, 1963 (also published in *World Marxist Review*, March, 1963), and March 30, 1963.

tivized; industrial administration substantially decentralized; workers' control, and local and republican autonomy, had also modified earlier centralism; Marxist doctrine had been revised distinctively, although by official action rather than individual freedom of interpretation; greater cultural freedom and international interchange lessened the party's control of the arts and scholarship; the continuing cult of Tito's personality was combined with a genuine collective leadership and broader public participation. As we have noted above, the initial reaction to the Congress, although positive, was circumspect, and for some time Belgrade held a watching brief on the progress of de-Stalinization, particularly in the neighbouring communist states.

Paradoxically, the *rapprochement* with the Soviet Union in the spring of 1962, coincided with a substantial tightening up of the Yugoslav system. After Tito's speech at Split in May, there ensued an enhancement of the role of the League of Communists as the directing force of Yugoslav society, as well as an intensification of its own unity and discipline; a reversion to stricter centralist control of the economy; a reassertion of the need for a single national economy and rejection of "localism" or "republican narrow-mindedness"; and an emphasis on a common Yugoslav national feeling as opposed to the more restricted nationalism associated with the individual republics and their dominant nationalities.[15] Simultaneous with this trend towards greater centralism and unity were the trial and re-imprisonment of Djilas, for the publication of his book *Conversations with Stalin*, ostensibly for revealing official data and, as the verdict put it, "warming up the campaign of slander against Yugoslavia." These measures were interpreted by some Western observers as closely associated with the *rapprochement* with the U.S.S.R. and were indeed cited by Khrushchev as corrections of previous errors, which thereby justified his own policy of accord with Yugoslavia.[16] It is likely that these actions were taken

[15]For Tito's speech, *Borba*, May 7, 1962. See also speech by Ranković at the Central Committee, *ibid.*, July 23, 1962; Tito's speech at the Congress of People's Youth, *ibid.*, Jan. 24, 1963.

[16]Speech to the Supreme Soviet during Tito's visit, *Izvestiya*, Dec. 13, 1962, and *Borba*, Dec. 13, 1962.

largely to meet the economic crisis and did not mean an abandonment of the specifically Yugoslav "path to socialism." Even the imprisonment of Djilas seems to have represented not so much a "sacrifice" to Moscow as a reaction to what was regarded as his provocative behaviour that was causing embarrassment and resentment to his former colleagues in the leadership. Nonetheless these departures from the distinctive Yugoslav pattern of communism certainly created a climate more favourable for the *rapprochement* with the U.S.S.R., which was dictated in any case by considerations of foreign policy.

The process of de-Stalinization in Eastern Europe has been uneven and spasmodic, and has probably not run its full course. The attack on Stalinism was bound to generate hopes and demands for greater freedom among all the Eastern European peoples, and where these ambitions were not satisfied, to produce renewed frustration and discontent. The purges in Bulgaria and Hungary and still more, the ferment in Czechoslovakia, coming as that did almost two years later and in a country long notorious for its passivity, suggested the long-term implications of the Congress for the whole of Eastern Europe. There is no reason to be surprised if continuing factional struggles and group pressures produce further delayed reactions elsewhere. Although the effect of a complete break between China and the Soviet Union on the course of de-Stalinization is difficult to predict, it seems likely to weaken the position of those communists who have looked to Peking for support in their resistance to de-Stalinization and to encourage others to respond to deep-seated popular desires for a more radical elimination of the worst features of Stalinism.

The analysis of de-Stalinization is a complicated matter, which has not been fully explored above. Stalinism is itself a complex phenomenon, embracing, not only the despotic rule of one man, the cult of his personality, and the terror and police methods associated with his rule and that of his prototypes in Eastern Europe, but also certain key features of communism as developed by Stalin and imitated in the satellites, including, for instance, centalized planning and industrial management, collectivized agriculture, party control of culture, and the bureaucratization of the party. Correspondingly, the negation of Stalinism, or de-Stalinization, is not something easily measured. Certainly the mere removal of statues or pictures, or even the verbal denigration of Stalin and his counterparts elsewhere, do not provide an accurate index of progress. The U.S.S.R. itself has carried through only partial de-Stalinization, and retains in greater or lesser degree certain essential traits of the old system. In the same way, in Eastern Europe, some countries have moved faster and further than others, and have changed more in certain respects than in others. For each of the major aspects of Stalinism, there is a spectrum of change in Eastern Europe, the individual country, including the U.S.S.R., occupying a different point on each scale. Nor is the position fixed, as official policies move in one or other direction from time to time.

Discussion of de-Stalinization does not exhaust the problem of analysing the heterogeneity of communism. A more precise measure of the national distinctiveness of the Eastern European states, including the U.S.S.R., might be better attained by comparing and contrasting them, not with Stalinism, but with each other in respect of individual features of the communist model, such as continuity of leadership; degree of personal absolutism; cult of personality; extent of terror; and of party and governmental democracy; the degree of intellectual freedom; of ideological distinctiveness; of centralization of the economy; and of collectivization of agriculture. For each of these items, an individual country may be placed at some point on a continuum, the position occupied varying on each scale, and fluctuating with changing circumstances. For instance, in intellectual freedom, the gamut would run from Poland (greatest) at one extreme to Albania (least) at the other; in continuity of leadership from Albania, East Germany, and Rumania (greatest) to the U.S.S.R., Poland, and Hungary (least); in collectivization of agriculture, from the U.S.S.R. (greatest) to Poland and Yugoslavia (least); in terror, from Albania or Czechoslovakia (greatest) to Poland (least); in ideological distinctiveness, from Albania (most Stalinist or dogmatist) to Yugoslavia (most revisionist). None of these scales of variation would be easy to construct, or exact in definition, but such an attempt would afford a more realistic image of the mosaic of national communism than our present impressionistic sketches.

Finally, it should be noted that the categories of national differentiation do not coincide at all with the classification according to degree of freedom from Soviet control. The struggle for external autonomy was, for instance, not necessarily correlated with internal thaw. Albania and Yugoslavia, although both independent, stand at opposite extremes according to most of the above criteria of differentiation. Departure from the bloc does not necessarily involve (*vide* Albania) fundamental and immediate changes in domestic policies and institutions, nor does it exclude (*vide* Yugoslavia) later shifts towards closer association with, and greater approximation to, the U.S.S.R. Nor does continued membership in the bloc rule out considerable experimentation in the ways of communism or significant striving for autonomy. Poland, which is less free of Soviet influence than Yugoslavia, has shown in certain respects greater diversity from the Soviet pattern than the latter. Czechoslovakia and Hungary, although both extremely dependent on the Soviet Union, differ greatly from each other and from her, the former in being more, and the latter less, Stalinist in spirit. Rumania, Stalinist to the core, has shown marked evidence of independence of action, while East Germany, equally Stalinist, remains devoid of such a tendency. None of the tendencies have persisted without modifications in the past, and none will remain unchanged in the future. The theme of national communism will continue to be answered by the counter-themes of Soviet influence and of communist uniformity, in an ever modulating counterpoint, defying any rigid or schematic analysis. The aftermath of the XXII Congress clearly suggests that national communism in the various forms here described is likely to intensify rather than to decline in the future, and that it remains a complex and kaleidoscopic force that must ever be reckoned with in our analysis of communism in Eastern Europe and the world.

3

TWO UNORTHODOX SATELLITES*

IT MAY SEEM PARADOXICAL to place in the same category of the "unorthodox" two communist states, Poland and Hungary, which have presumably experienced such a different fate since 1956. The world has become accustomed to recognizing that Poland, since that critical year, has followed an unusual course in comparison with its fellow satellites in Eastern Europe. Although some of the experimentation of the period after 1956 has been modified or abandoned, there remain important respects in which the victories of that year have been preserved. The world has tended to have a very different image of post-1956 Hungary and to write it off as a new and even more distasteful form of Stalinism, imposed on an unwilling country by the brute force of Soviet arms. It has not been sufficiently realized that, in spite of the defeat of the revolution in 1956, those tragic events were not without some positive gains, at least in terms of the destruction of the old system, and that in more recent years Hungary has distinguished itself from other members of the Soviet bloc by a certain willingness to experiment with new ideas and methods. A dynamic analysis suggests that whereas Poland has made a partial retreat from the high point of autonomy and nonconformity in 1956, Hungary has effected a noticeable advance in the direction of a nationally distinctive form of communism, thus bringing the two countries somewhat closer together in the spectrum of world communism. Not surprisingly, when the XXII Congress of the Communist party of the

*Published in *International Journal*, XVIII, No. 1 (Winter, 1962–63).

Soviet Union in 1961 produced the renewed onslaught on Stalin and Stalinism, it was nowhere greeted with more enthusiasm than in Hungary and Poland.

That there remain important differences between Polish and Hungarian communism cannot be denied. The swift drive towards the goal of complete collectivization of agriculture in Hungary, for instance, contrasts sharply with the maintenance of private peasant farming in Poland. This, and other differences, should not be allowed to hide important aspects common to both countries, differentiating them from other more orthodox satellites. If the standard of orthodoxy is Stalinism, then, apart from Poland, no communist country had moved further from that odious system than Hungary by the end of 1961, so that the XXII Congress, although warmly welcomed, did not produce any spectacular immediate consequences. The worst aspects of Stalinism had already been destroyed, as in Poland, in 1956, and further measures of de-Stalinization were not as urgently necessary as elsewhere. Symbolic of this fact was the huge marble base of the former Stalin statue in Budapest, which has remained empty following its destruction in the October days. Even if the standard of orthodoxy is taken to be present Soviet practices, the greater willingness, and ability, of Poland to depart from the Soviet pattern in significant respects should not exclude the recognition that Hungary, although in the main hewing to a course similar to that of the Soviet Union under Khrushchev, has adopted some procedures more "Polish" than "Russian" in character.

The most important single factor distinguishing these two from the other states in the bloc and explaining contemporary similarities is the experience of 1956. Only Poland and Hungary have undergone the trauma of witnessing the full collapse of communism in its Stalinist form in a crisis of national dimensions during which party leaders, spurred on by rank and file dissatisfaction and revisionist thinking, took the course of open resistance to Soviet policy and launched a claim for a new form of communism and a freer relationship with the Soviet Union. Why events such as these occurred only in

Hungary and in Poland, and were not duplicated in other communist countries is a complicated question of historical analysis which this essay cannot begin to discuss. Suffice it to say that in both countries the particularly hateful form taken by communism under Stalinist dispensation generated a will to resist, shared by communists as well as non-communists, and nourished by an ancient record of hostility towards the Soviet Union and its Tsarist predecessor, a deep tradition of militant and conservative nationalism, a long-standing Western intellectual and cultural orientation, and profound religious attachments, chiefly to Roman Catholicism. The close integration of the two states with the Soviet bloc, and even the presence of Soviet troops on their territory, were not enough to counteract the powerful currents of resistance that culminated in open outburst in the autumn of 1956.

The ultimate outcome was significantly different, almost diametrically so, with the revolt in Poland guided into channels of compromise by local leaders who remained in control of events, and that in Hungary escaping from such control, bursting into open national revolution, and finally being crushed by Soviet military intervention. Nonetheless, in spite of this divergent sequel, the events of 1956 continue to exercise a profound impact on the consciousness of both peoples and both leaderships, and go far to explain the substantial degree of similarity of outlook some years later. The lesson of 1956 remains vivid in the minds of Polish and Hungarian leaders. For both, the central political purpose pursued since that time has been to rebuild, on the ruins of Stalinism, a system of communism more stable and viable than that which had crumbled in those days. Force alone was evidently not enough to maintain communism among an unwilling and hostile people. There had to be a refashioning of communism in somewhat more decent and acceptable forms and a reshaping of relations with the Soviet Union on the basis of a greater degree of autonomy and less direct Soviet control over domestic affairs.

This has meant a "middle course" between two extremes.

On the one hand, both régimes have sought to maintain at least the major "gains of October," and in particular to avoid a reversion to the evils of Stalinism which would surely generate increasing resistance and an ultimate breakdown of the system anew. On the other hand, both have sought to avoid too great a relaxation or liberalization, which might cause the recurrence of the "fever" of which Khrushchev once spoke, and from which they had, as if by a miracle, recovered. The slogan of a "war on two fronts," against "Stalinism" and "liberalism," or as the Moscow conferences of 1957 and 1960 put it, against "dogmatism" and "revisionism," had therefore a substantial reality in both Hungary and Poland. Since Khrushchev himself, in pursuing his "controlled reform" in the Soviet Union and in the bloc as a whole, seemed also to be seeking to avoid these twin evils, the Hungarian and Polish régimes saw in the Soviet leader their surest support, and were anxious to offer their own aid and comfort to him in his struggle against opponents at home and in other countries of the bloc.

To accomplish this delicate operation of sailing between Scylla and Charybdis, Poland and Hungary possessed leaders well suited for this task and not entirely without resemblance in personality and experience. Gomułka and Kádár were men of working-class origin, without extensive education or intellectual pretensions. Both had been, throughout their adult lives, "true believers," dedicating themselves with courage and at personal cost to the cause of communism. Both were men devoted to the Soviet Union as the leader of world communism and normally ready to obey its commands without serious question. Both were, however, "home communists" who had not been closely associated with the Comintern and had spent the war years in their own countries. Under Stalinism in its post-war phase, both had been brought to oppose prevailing concepts of communism, and had suffered long terms of imprisonment at the hands of their more subservient comrades. During the post-Stalin thaw, both had shown themselves ready, Gomułka more so than Kádár, to associate themselves with currents of reform within communism. Although neither was a "national communist" in the extreme sense of a Tito or a

Nagy, both saw the need for some degree of national autonomy and differentiation of the individual members of the communist bloc, while maintaining the closest association with the Soviet Union and substantial conformity with its policies. In particular during and after 1956, both recognized that communism could survive only if it pursued a middle road that would avoid the worst mistakes of the old system and at the same time the danger of excessive relaxation or reform.

True, Gomułka had come to power as a symbol and leader of Polish resistance to Soviet claims, whereas Kádár had been placed in his position by Soviet bayonets and his more "Polish" associate, Nagy, was executed. Once in power, however, the tasks of the two leaders, and the methods used, showed marked similarity. Both were men of simple and modest nature, opposed to display and personal aggrandizement, and well suited to give effect to a new course designed to replace the cult of personality. Although, like other communist leaders, both exercise supreme power, these two live modestly and rule quietly, presumably leaning much on the advice of their close associates, and encouraging no sycophantic adulation of their own persons. In neither country does one see the picture of the leader prominently displayed in offices and other public places. Without possessing the gift of eloquence, or other charismatic attributes, Kádár and Gomułka are not without leadership ability, and are capable of generating a pragmatic loyalty from their followers and even of winning from their opponents a certain grudging admission of their ability and human decency. In Hungary, for instance, non-communists express the view that Kádár has accomplished something of a "miracle" in gaining a reluctant acquiescence on the part of a population with plenty of reason to regard him with hatred as a foreign-imposed puppet.

In each country the Communist party continues to be the main instrument of political rule, dominating every aspect of life, and mobilizing its members to support and fulfil the current line of policy. As highly centralized as ever, the party confers the main power of decision-making on its top organs, especially the Presidium, while urging all its members and lower organs to take a more active part in the discussion of party affairs under the leadership of the centre. The most significant change has occurred in personnel, both at the top and at the middle and lower levels of the apparatus. In both Poland and Hungary, the "war on two fronts" has meant weeding out from positions of power the exponents of the extremes of dogmatism and revisionism. In theory, the latter was regarded as the greater danger, involving viewpoints which were un-Marxist or even anti-Marxist, and which had prepared the ground, especially in Hungary, for the "counter-revolution" against communism, whereas the dogmatists, although misguided, were considered loyal Marxists who had committed grievous "errors" during the Stalinist period. Gradually, however, the campaigns against revisionism and dogmatism came to be more and more expediently treated, with the leadership occupying a position midway between the two extremes, and emphasizing the danger of one or the other in accordance with the special circumstances of the country and the time.

In Poland, the party has remained firmly in the hands of the "centrists" of the Gomułka persuasion ever since October, 1956. The main Stalinists have long since been removed from power, although some remained in positions of influence. Having settled the Stalinist problem early, the Polish régime paid increasing attention to the revisionists, who, although tolerated more than in Hungary, were regarded with suspicion as persons who wished to advance further on the road to reform. They have been under even more intensive attack since 1956 and have not had any significant role in the exercise of power since that time. More and more they have been disillusioned by the retreats and consolidation of the Gomułka régime. Dogmatism has remained a problem, especially in the apparatus of the party, but not one that causes serious concern.

In Hungary, the revisionists have been regarded even more intolerantly as the real culprits of 1956. Since the execution of Nagy, there has been no room for any of his associates or supporters in the seats of power, and no desire on their part to associate themselves with the Kádár régime. After the XXII

Congress, Kádár went out of his way to make clear that there would be no rehabilitation of those who had opposed communism in 1956 and no "liberalization" of the party. It became increasingly clear, however, that of the "horseflies" to left and right, as Kádár picturesquely termed them, the ones on the left, the so-called dogmatists, were more serious threats to the centrist leadership. Although revisionism remained a grave problem among writers and intellectuals, the real obstacle to the implementation of the more moderate course advocated by Kádár was the dogmatism of the party veterans who found it difficult to adapt themselves to the new methods. The XXII Congress encouraged Kádár to shift the emphasis of the two-front struggle from revisionism to dogmatism. In the programmatic principles published in preparation for the party congress in 1962, the danger of revisionism was soft-pedalled, indeed hardly mentioned, and dogmatism or sectarianism was made the main target. Even more significant was the removal of Kiss and Marosan from the Politburo, and the somewhat more symbolic exclusion from the party of Rákosi and Gerö, long since removed from the seats of power.

Second only to the determination of both Hungarian and Polish leaders to assure the dominance of the centrist wing of the party has been their desire to win greater public support. The experience of 1956 had laid bare the weakness of the party, and had forced them to realize, as Kádár was ready to say publicly, that the majority of the population was, and would remain, non-communist or non-Marxist. If the régime were to rule, and to rule effectively, it must therefore reach some kind of accommodation with the non-communist masses, and it must rely on something other than force, as in the "bad days," to secure obedience. In Poland this led to the revival of other parties, playing a minor role, but performing a useful function; an improvement in the procedures of elections, without, of course, permitting the possibility of a communist defeat; an enlivening of parliamentary discussions, especially in committees, and above all, the uneasy agreement between the state and the Catholic Church. Less well known is the parallel effort of the Hungarian régime to revitalize the National Front and to appeal for non-communist support. "He who is not against us is with us," runs the present slogan, justifying the abandonment of traditional hostility towards all non-communists and their exclusion from any participation in public affairs. More recently, Kádár has urged the communist régime to act as though there were a multi-party system and a "daily secret vote." The action of rehabilitating Count Károlyi, socialist Premier of Hungary in 1919, and one-time post-war ambassador to France, and of re-burying his remains in ceremonial fashion in Budapest, was part of this effort to popularize the idea of the desirability of association of non-communist and communist in a revitalized National Front, an idea for which Károlyi, it was said, at certain times stood. This has not meant, any more than in Poland, the party relinquishing its exclusive leadership, and there have been no appointments of non-communists to important positions at the centre. At the lower and middle levels of government, however, the effort to secure the participation of non-communists in public affairs has been pressed with sufficient vigour to alienate older communists of more radical persuasion.

Nor has this policy been without success in affecting the attitude of non-communists towards the régime. Popular opposition to communism remains widespread, and political apathy a marked characteristic of the population. The position of the régime in both Hungary and Poland has, however, long been strengthened by the fact that it represents the "only alternative." The experience of 1956 rules out the possibility of a non-communist system under present circumstances. Even a much more liberalized communism is not conceivable in the forseeable future. A reversion to Stalinism, or physical occupation by the Soviet Union, are regarded as extremes to be avoided at any cost. A new realism that has existed for some time in Poland, has appeared in Hungary, too, based on the necessity of reckoning with the existence of the present semi-liberal régime for some time to come, and on the recognition of it as a "lesser evil" to any other alternative. Kádár, like Gomułka, is viewed as the main safeguard against a return of Rákosi and Stalinism, and even as a bulwark against Chinese communism. The XXII Congress strengthened this assumption, placing Khrushchev, as well as Kádár, in a favourable light, and engendering an increasing hopefulness about the future.

The visitor to Hungary in 1962 was surprised to observe not only this moderate optimism about the future but a note of positive engagement among non-communists, not unlike that found among some Poles. The course of wisdom, it was argued, was to reconcile oneself to the present "house" of Hungary, rather than seek alternative habitation which was not available, and to help modestly to improve it as a place of residence. This argument in favour of some form of accommodation with the present régime and against the traditional unconditional rejection was given powerful expression by the noted writer, Lászlo Nemeth, in his play, *The Journey*, presented publicly in Budapest. Nemeth treated the problem with considerable frankness in a manner that could not but be discomfiting to many communists. His positive heroes were not the old-line Stalinist, nor the staunch non-compromising opponent of the régime, but the non-communist professor, who, after a visit to the Soviet Union, was willing to seek a basis for understanding with the powers that be, and the decent communist who did not take unfair advantage of this concession. This represents not so much an ideological *rapprochement* such as that favoured by a few Poles, including even certain Catholics, but rather the pragmatic or "geo-political" viewpoint widely held in Poland, which accepts the necessity of co-operation, without love or emotional loyalty, with the system as it now exists, and entertains a modest hope that this may contribute to a progressive humanization of it. Whereas in Poland this realism has developed out of an earlier mood of radical and utopian hopes, in Hungary it represents a recovery from the nadir of hopelessness of the years after 1956.

The visitor to Hungary was also struck by an atmosphere of apparent freedom to meet and talk with foreigners. The old fear was to a large extent gone, one was told. The risks attached to independent thought and open discussion were much fewer than before. To publish was, of course, much more difficult. But Hungarians pride themselves on being the "second freest" country in the Soviet bloc, and there seems to be some truth to their claim. True, there is much less opportunity for public dissent than in Poland. There has been no Club of the Crooked Circle, which was, until early 1962, the scene of controversial discussions in Warsaw. There has been no extensive opportunity to travel and study abroad, such as that made possible by the Ford Foundation grants to Polish scholars. Nor, above all, has there been a special position for the Catholic Church, free, as in Poland, to state an alternative faith and to carry on a dialogue of mutual criticism with the temporal power. Hungarian Catholicism is not as vital a force, with its primate still confined within the United States Embassy, and lesser churchmen not in a position to challenge the state ideology. Nor do the Catholics possess, as in Poland, their own university, their press and clubs, and parliamentary representatives, able, within strict limits, to present an alternative point of view. In Hungary, however, prominent noncommunist writers of ability are writing again, after a self-imposed silence, are published and widely read, and present therefore a counterbalance to the régime similar in some ways to the Church in Poland. Foreign literature, in translation, is more readily available, especially in a journal published for this purpose. A celebration of an anniversary of Robert Burns in the spring of 1962, at the British Embassy, attracted more than one hundred prominent Budapesters, including several well-known poets. The hand of orthodoxy still lies heavy on much of Hungarian scholarship, which seems somewhat cut off, not only from the West, but also from the Soviet Union and its fellow "people's democracies." Nonetheless, cultural and intellectual contacts with the outside world are warmly sought after by scholars, and their conversation and their libraries reveal a considerable familiarity with Western currents of thought and research.

This remains but a modest advance in contrast to Poland, whose intellectual life is unique in the communist world for its liveliness and lack of conformism. The Polish intellectuals enjoy a substantial freedom unknown elsewhere in the bloc.

In the main, Polish intellectuals must accept the system and the Marxist framework of thought, although those of Catholic viewpoint may reject Marxism while expressing loyalty to the system. Diversity of view between Catholics and Marxists, and among the Marxists themselves, exists, and has some opportunity for public expression. The doors to the West are open in an intellectual sense, and Western scholarship is well known, through personal contact as well as through the printed word. Even a most orthodox scholar, such as the philosopher Adam Schaff, carries on a dialogue with Western scholars, and even with Polish exiles and Radio Free Europe, that is hardly conceivable elsewhere. Equally unusual was the "debate" on the nature and conditions of intellectual freedom carried on in 1962 in the daily press, with some participants arguing the case for absolute intellectual freedom, even in the social sciences. Others set the limits more narrowly, asserting the need for acceptance of limitations of a political kind by all scholars, and, for Marxists and party members, admitting freedom only "within Marxism." Although the debate has not led to a fundamental shift in the direction of an open society, it is indicative of the deeper aspirations of Polish scholars, even of Marxist persuasion.

It is in fact interesting to compare the role of Marxism as a doctrine in Poland and Hungary, and to observe marked differences as well as resemblances. Marxism as an ideology has lost some of its hold, but is by no means dead. Both Kádár and Gomułka are pragmatists, not ideologues, and realities rather than theories play the main part in decision-making. In both countries, the events of Stalinism and of 1956 produced a breakdown of Marxist faith, especially among the youth, as clearly revealed by a poll of student opinion in Warsaw in 1958. The ferment of pre-1956 and post-1956 radical revisionism has largely died down in Poland, and official attacks on such deviations from orthodoxy have steadily increased. None the less Marxism seems more alive in Poland than in Hungary, perhaps because of the contacts with Western scholarship and the conflict with Catholicism, which have forced Polish Marxists to develop a more reasoned and reasonable defence of their faith. Marxists of intellectual stature, such as Adam Schaff and Oscar Lange, stand relatively high in party circles, and are capable of infusing into official doctrine elements of originality and interest, even while defending it against more radical innovators such as the philosopher, Kołakowski. In the presence of such persons one cannot seriously assert that Marxism is dead, or that it has remained entirely dogmatic, even though its hold on the youth, and its impact on policy, may be relatively slight.

In Hungary there was no comparable ferment among Marxists, even before 1956, and after the revolution no opportunity for raising serious revisionist ideas. The eminent philosopher, George Lukács, a much more orthodox Marxist than, say, Kołakowski in Poland, although closely associated with Nagy in the October days, now lives and works freely in Budapest, and publishes abroad, in German and English, his works on aesthetics and culture. He is no longer the target of fierce official attack. His influence, however, is minimal, as his works are not available in Magyar, and his activities are limited to his own research and writing, without the opportunity for a public exposition of his views. Nor are there any Hungarian counterparts for the Polish "orthodox" revisionists, such as Lange, and in particular no opposite number for Schaff, as a capable "manager" of intellectual affairs, equally conversant with the West and the Soviet East, and able to conduct a debate with his opponents abroad with some sophistication. In Hungary, the cultural boss, Kallai, with aides such as Adam Wirth, Nemes and Szirmai, carries on a stereotyped struggle against what he calls "kulak" ideas, with great accent on the need for party-mindedness or *partiinost*. A Marxist of prominence, Erik Molnar, once holding high office under Rákosi, continues to be an important figure in Hungarian scholarship, as head of the Institute of History, although lacking the political authority of a Schaff. In 1959 Molnar stood his ground firmly against critics of his book on the development of Western capitalism, and vigorously argued later that in the intellectual sphere dogmatism is the greatest danger.

Sociology also provides an interesting case study of the differences, and yet some similarity, between the two countries. In Poland, with the decline of the dominating position of dialectical materialism after 1956, sociology experienced a notable revival as a field of research. Contemporary American sociology has not been without some influence, in particular in the stimulus to undertake empirical studies, such as public opinion measurement, and many Polish sociologists have visited or studied in the United States in recent years. A criticism of the "mania" of poll-taking by Adam Schaff met with sharp response from Polish scholars defending the value of such techniques of investigation. Soviet philosophers have shown a keen interest in Polish developments, to the extent of sending observers to Poland and receiving a top-level delegation of Polish sociologists in Moscow for seminar discussions. In broader debates concerning the desirability of a centre for sociological studies in the bloc as a whole, Polish and Soviet scholars found themselves in substantial agreement and received some support from the Hungarians. In Hungarian scholarship, it is true, sociology still does not exist as a field in its own right. One sociologist, Sandor Szalai, was indeed rudely criticized by party organs for advocating the use of American empirical methods. Nonetheless, there is an interest in concrete studies, even in party circles, and of all countries of the Soviet bloc, apart from Poland, Hungary has shown herself more responsive to this trend.

How are these distinctive trends of Polish and Hungarian domestic affairs related to the position of the two countries in the Soviet orbit and to their attitude towards the Soviet Union as its leader? Hungary and Poland remain fully integrated in the bloc, and are participants in the conferences of Communist parties. Both are members of the Warsaw Pact, and continue to have Soviet troops stationed on their soil. Both are members of Comecon and subject to the ever increasing unification of the economies of its members. It is, however, impossible to explain their domestic divergence from other members merely in terms of dictation from Moscow, especially in the case of Poland. Poland enjoys what might be called a status of semi-independence, going back to her successful resistance to Soviet pressure in 1956. The course then adopted was clearly an independent Polish initiative, accepted with reluctance by the U.S.S.R. as the only solution short of military intervention. Although the later retrenchment may have been due in part to Soviet pressure, in the main it must be considered as a recognition by the Polish leadership itself of the desirability of some withdrawal from the advanced position of 1956. Moreover the retreat has been partial only, and in certain respects, notably in relation to private farming, the Church, and the matters discussed in this chapter, there is still a distinctive Polish path.

The deviations of Hungary from the straight and narrow path of traditional communism may perhaps more easily be interpreted as concessions to Soviet pressure. Kádár, by virtue of the circumstances of his installation in power, is more dependent on the Soviet Union and less likely to resist her will in important matters. Like all members of the bloc, however, Hungary now enjoys a certain degree of freedom of manoeuvre within the Soviet orbit, unknown in Stalin's time, and may in fact be using this freedom to follow a course of action dictated by her own conception of what is required if a new 1956 is to be averted.

For both Kádár and Gomułka the XXII Congress represented a heartening development, suggesting a continuation and a reassertion of the Khrushchev line of reform and relaxation, and endorsing anew their own course of cautious change. As far as was known Hungary and Poland gave full support to Khrushchev and the Soviet party in the conflict with China and Albania and showed no sign of sympathy for either of the dissidents. Indeed, fear of China and her extreme form of communism, not to mention her more reckless attitude in matters of peace and war, solidified still further their closeness with the Soviet Union as a barrier against a more distasteful form of communism, reminiscent of Stalinism, and with Khrushchev as a spokesman for peaceful coexistence and a pragmatic searcher for a solution of international tensions. Albania, although treated more with contempt than fear, also typified a reversion to the old ways of rule. Although Khrushchev's treatment of Albania smacked of old-style Stalinist domineering over the satellites, both Poles and Hungarians accepted it as a necessary method of combatting a challenge to the new pattern of communism represented by Khrushchev and themselves. Both were also willing to go along with the *rapprochement* with Yugoslavia, a course harder for Hungary in view of Tito's role during the 1956 events, but now accepted as a condition of a more liberal course in the bloc.

Khrushchev could hardly fail to appreciate the ready response to his policies in Budapest and Warsaw. Both were weak points in the entire Soviet power structure in 1956, and have not by any means fully recovered from the effects of that year. The legacy of those events can only be counteracted by a policy of carefully regulated reform which does not endanger the régimes by unloosing forces difficult to control, but rather strengthens them by widening the base of public support. Kádár combines utter loyalty to Moscow with a certain degree of public acceptance by Hungarians, which seems to be increasing as time goes on. Gomułka, some of whose policies may awaken misgivings in Moscow, moves with relative circumspection and has won a more widespread body of popular support. In both countries, Khrushchev can count on leaders who strongly believe in the rightness of the course he is now pursuing and who need his backing to carry through their own variant of it at home.

For Moscow, the primary goal is the maintenance of a unified and loyal bloc. Insubordination on matters of bloc relations, foreign policies, and ideology cannot, as the Albanian case demonstrated, be tolerated. As long as the states of the Soviet bloc guarantee both loyalty and their own stability, a considerable diversity in domestic patterns may be tolerated and even encouraged. In countries such as Czechoslovakia or Rumania, where no 1956 created an urgent need for substantial measures of de-Stalinization, a more conservative and cautious stance may for the time being be accepted, as long as it does not conceal sympathies with Stalinist tendencies in bloc politics and does not involve the danger of defection on the crucial matters of ideology and foreign relations. In the long run, however, the Poles and Hungarians offer to all a model of cautious liberalization capable of maintaining stability, assuring loyalty, and widening the foundations of public approval.

4

TWO ORTHODOX SATELLITES *

IN A TIME of increasing communist heterodoxy, Bulgaria and Rumania for long remained models of loyalty to the Soviet bloc and of conformity with Soviet policies. Neither Bulgaria, with less than 8,000,000 people, nor even Rumania, with nearly 18,000,000, was in a position to offer serious resistance to Soviet pressure, even if they should have so desired. Geographically close to the Soviet Union, and entirely surrounded, in the case of Rumania, by communist states, and in that of Bulgaria, by traditional enemies, neither possessed the freedom of manoeuvre enjoyed by less exposed bloc members. The absence of Soviet troops, withdrawn from Rumania as recently as 1958, hardly freed them from the military threat of their giant neighbour. Both were countries less than a century removed from Turkish rule, and in the few war-ridden decades of independence, neither was able to fashion a just and stable political community. Both have had little tradition of democratic governance, having succumbed to local dictatorships between the wars, their democratic parties having been discredited by weakness and by association with Nazi Germany. Both were, in 1944, at the time of communist take-over, extremely underdeveloped economically, and backward in their social policies, their small working class and their predominant peasantry living at low standards. Under communist rule, both experienced a particularly ruthless and violent form of political domination, and reacted with minimal

*Published in *International Journal*, XVII, No. 4 (Autumn, 1962).

changes to the course of de-Stalinization launched by Khrushchev since 1955.

Yet it would be folly to ignore the differences even between these two orthodox satellites. "Bulgaria is not Rumania," said a member of the Bulgarian Central Committee in conversation with the author in Sofia. Three weeks of travel supplemented by study confirmed for this writer the truth of such a statement. The experience of the past warns us against the danger of treating the communist states as uniform and of ignoring their concrete and distinctive features.

The capital cities, somewhat symbolically, stand in marked contrast to each other. Bucharest, set in the midst of the flat Wallachian plain, about forty miles from the Danube to the south or the Carpathians to the north, enjoys a less attractive location than Sofia, on its high plateau, with nearby Mount Vitosha often snow-capped, and the more distant Balkan mountains visible. Bucharest, however, with its broad avenues, and spacious parks, even with an Arc de Triomphe, has retained some of the Parisian look of which it has long boasted. With its handsome modern architecture, it is unique in the Soviet bloc, although it also possesses a huge skyscraper of Stalinesque design, the printing house of *Scinteia*, the party organ. Its traffic is heavier than that of most East European capitals, and deafens the ears with its cacophony of honking. Sofia is much smaller and quieter, less Western and modern, and retains somewhat more evidence of its Byzantine and Turkish past. Its not unhandsome nineteenth-century public buildings, low and charming, have been dwarfed by a new city centre of heavy grey monolithic structures unlike anything in Moscow for ugliness or grimness. Even its main downtown streets are drab in comparison with the smart glitter of Bucharest. Away from the centre, of course, both cities are poor and shabby, but great uniform apartment houses are gradually replacing the shacks and slums of the past.

The countryside is more uniform, but with the inevitable differences of scenery, cultivation, dwellings, and dress of two distinctive national communities. Bulgaria is a kind of smaller version of Rumania, with the plain of the Maritza replacing the great Danubian plain, the Rhodope and Balkan mountain ranges taking the place of the Carpathians, and the striking Black Sea resorts near Varna the counterpart of those at Constanza. On both sides of the Danube, the common border, the tiny farm cottages and sheds of yesterday contrast with the large new buildings of the collective or state farms, and the tractor stations. In Wallachia, to the north, the old houses, tiny and primitive, are often made of wattle and mud, sometimes with bricks at the base or under the roof, which is often thatched. The side to the north is flat and windowless, on the south stands a columned veranda, with Turkish arches and pictorial decoration. In Dobrogea, to the south, the typical Bulgarian farm house appears, small, brick or white-washed, with red tiled roofs, crude woven fences, and picket gates. On the Rumanian side, the roads were crowded with small, covered wagons, and oxen-drawn carts, and on the Bulgarian side, with tiny, low carts, pulled by small burros. Everywhere, people were at work in the fields, more often than not with hoe or sickle, or sleeping at the roadside in the full sunlight. Here and there, a huge old-fashioned combine was at work, or more often, stood idle and rusty in the open farm yard. On both sides of the border, herdsmen, young children or old folks, endlessly watched or drove a herd of sheep, or cows, water-buffalo or horses, more often a single cow or two. At dusk, the highway was alive with animals wending their way homeward. Everywhere, on both sides, peasants, weary and poor, sometimes in patchwork clothing, sometimes in native costume, looked as they might have looked a century ago. It was hard to believe that these were countries on the verge of entering the "affluent" society of "communism!" Yet the wealth was there—wheat, sunflowers, cattle, and in Bulgaria, roses and tobacco; in Rumania, timber and oil.

Both countries are largely Orthodox in religion, but as in Russia, the subordination of Church to State has presented no serious problem. In Rumania, the Greek Catholics, or Uniates, were in 1948 absorbed by the Orthodox Church, after centuries of separation. Churches in the villages are few, and in the city not well attended. A more serious religious problem presents itself in Rumania in the large Hungarian minority in Transylvania, who are Catholic, Calvinist, or Unitarian. Indeed the nationality question, represented by almost two and a half million non-Rumanians, including more than a million and a half Hungarians, and almost 400,000 Germans, is a unique feature of Rumanian society, distinguishing it from all other European bloc members. Most serious is the large Hungarian minority of Transylvania, a fact which does not make for the best of relations with Hungary, and contributes thereby to Rumania's dependence on the Soviet Union. Hungarian irredentism is by no means dead, although, of course, officially disavowed, and Rumania, without Transylvania, would be an impotent fragment.

Rumanian communists have avoided the error of their predecessors and have sought to achieve a coexistence of Rumanians and Hungarians by the recognition of the cultural rights of the minority. There has been no forced denationalization, and the Magyar language is permitted in educational and cultural life. A Hungarian autonomous region, with its capital at Tirgu-Mures, enjoys as much, or as little, self-government as other regions. Cluj, the ancient Hungarian cultural centre, is outside this region, but remains half Hungarian in population and possesses a Hungarian opera and theatre, as well as newspapers, churches, and associations using Magyar. Street signs are in both languages. Education may be in Magyar, if so desired, in elementary and middle schools, and even in the University of Cluj. The once independent Hungarian Babes University in Cluj was in 1959 merged with the Rumanian Bolyai University, but is still organized in two sections, with five faculties mixed, and two (law and economics) purely Rumanian. Hungarian students may, if they wish, do most of their work in Hungarian, but are required to learn Rumanian and to take certain general courses given only in Rumanian. In elementary and secondary schools, a similar process is taking place, with mixed schools replacing the formerly Rumanian and Hungarian schools. The purpose of this is said to be to bring the two nationalities together and not to destroy Hungarian national identity. It is clear, however, that it is designed to meet the problem of the still strong nationalism of the Hungarians and to associate them more and more closely with the Rumanian majority.

The Turkish minority of six to seven hundred thousand in Bulgaria does not constitute a problem of such grave proportions. Here, too, however, the religious affiliation (Moslem) of the Turks complicates the ethnic diversity. Here, too, the official policy is to require the learning of the majority language and to wean the minority away from its national and religious separatism. Much more serious is the unacknowledged problem of the Macedonian community. Traditionally, and currently, the Bulgarians have refused to recognize the Macedonians as a separate nationality and have therefore not permitted educational or cultural life to be conducted in anything other than the Bulgarian language, of which Macedonian is considered merely a regional dialect. In Yugoslavia, on the contrary, the communist régime has from the beginning treated Macedonian as a distinct language, and the Macedonians as a separate nationality, enjoying the political status of a republic, and possessing a flourishing cultural and educational life in the Macedonian language. For Bulgarian communists, as for their predecessors, this whole area, as well as adjacent territories in Greece, are Bulgarian in population and rightfully Bulgarian in political affiliation. As long as Yugoslavia was ideologically and politically an outcaste, the acerbity of Bulgarian-Yugoslav relations was intensified by the territorial and national dispute concerning the Macedonians. Now that Soviet policy looks towards a *rapprochement* with Tito's régime, the Macedonian question must be played down officially in Bulgaria. Strong feelings continue to exist, however, on both sides of the political frontier, and the problem constitutes a standing source of friction.

The linguistic contrast between the two neighbouring lands is not without cultural and political importance. Bulgarian, a Slavic language, is written in Cyrillic; Rumanian is a Latin language, using Latin script. The similarity of Bulgarian and Russian is greater than that of almost any other two Slavic languages. Hence Bulgarians understand Russian without great difficulty, although they find it hard to learn accurately because of its subtle differentiation. But Russian is required in both elementary and secondary schools, and indeed has been compulsory in the latter since 1878. Rumanian, on the other hand, once also written in Cyrillic, has long since adopted the Latin style, and in vocabulary resembles Spanish or Italian. Although Russian has been taught in the schools since the war (since 1956, on an optional basis), it is not widely spoken, and French still predominates among the intelligentsia. In Bulgaria, German seems more widely known than French, although English is spoken by many graduates of the former American College in Sofia. In both countries English is the most studied Western language in schools and universities.

Probing more deeply into the past and the present, one finds additional reasons which would suggest the likelihood of a close relationship of Bulgaria and Russia. Between the two world wars, and during them, there was deep and unconditional hostility towards the Soviet Union on the part of the ruling classes and the régimes in both Bulgaria and Rumania, and in the case of the latter, active participation in the war against Russia on the side of Nazi Germany. For the Bulgarians, however, there is a much longer and richer tradition of friendship with Russia, in particular during the war of liberation against the Turks in 1877–78. At the Shipka Pass, in the Balkan Mountains, lie the graves of Russian soldiers who died in the decisive battle against the Turks and there stands a great monument to "eternal Russian-Bulgarian friendship." In Sofia there are the tangible symbols of the historic Russian role in the monument of Tsar Alexander II, now inscribed "To Our Brother Liberators," and the great church of many gilded domes, Alexander Nevsky, built in the early twentieth century as another tribute to the Russian nation. Although Rumania, too, secured Russian aid in the emancipation of the principalities of Wallachia and Moldavia from the Turks, the image of Russia as the liberator is much less vivid. Much more central to the Rumanian historical tradition in modern times is the union of these two provinces with Transylvania and Bessarabia as a result of the Paris Peace of 1919, and the loss of Bessarabia to the Soviet Union in 1940 and again in 1944.

The history of Bulgarian socialism might be expected also to bring communist Bulgaria closer to Soviet Russia than Rumania. Bulgarian socialism has a rich tradition and deep roots, represented in particular by its founder, Dimitar Blagoev, who was active in Russian Marxist circles in the eighties, and in Bulgaria stood for a conception of socialism closer to Leninism than to Western social democracy. Even before 1914, Bulgarian socialism had divided into two wings, the "narrows" and the "broads," resembling somewhat the Bolshevik-Menshevik division of Russian Marxism, with the more radical Blagoev wing predominant. Between the wars, Bulgarian communism was fortunate in having as its leader Georgi Dimitrov, a prominent figure in the Comintern, and of world-wide renown, who returned to Bulgaria in 1944 to direct the new régime. It is perhaps not surprising that the Bulgarians have adopted, and retained, the barbaric Russian custom of exhibiting the body of their former leader in a mausoleum in downtown Sofia.

The Rumanians can point to no such rich heritage, or to leaders of such distinction. In a nation of conservative political and intellectual outlook, Rumanian socialism was extremely weak before World War I. Even the intellectual founder of Rumanian Marxism, Dobrogeanu, is severely condemned now for serious deviations from the correct Marxist path. Between the wars, Rumanian communism, illegal, was led by a series of persons, all of whom have been accused of anti-Marxist policies. Although some of its leading personalities, notably Anna Pauker, had close connections with the Comintern, most of these were purged in the post-war years. Its present commanding figure, Gheorghe Gheorghiu-Dej, had no personal experience with the Comintern, as he spent the years from 1933 to 1944 in prison after a railway strike. He emerged from confinement in 1944 to take over control of a party that numbered perhaps a thousand members and was unquestionably the weakest in Eastern Europe. This weakness, and the lack of tradition and of a reliable leader, condemn the régime to feebleness of rule and to dependence on the Soviet Union for its maintenance in power.

Party leadership, a crucial factor in determining the character of a Communist party and its relationship with Moscow, follows a somewhat similar pattern in both countries, but with significant distinctions. Both high commands, after the war, were made up of men of humble origin; in the Rumanian case largely workers, such as Gheorghiu-Dej himself; in Bulgaria, mainly peasants, and of veterans hardened by illegal, revolutionary experience and prison sentences. The Bulgarians had many who had spent years in Russia; the Rumanians were somewhat more of the "home" variety. Neither were distinguished for their intellectual stature, nor had, with rare exceptions, more than the most elementary education. Both directorates suffered severe purges in the Stalin period, notably in the execution of Kostov in Bulgaria, in 1950, the imprisonment of Pauker and Vasile Luca in Rumania, in 1952, and the execution, *after* the death of Stalin, of a Rumanian of considerable intellectual ability, Patrascanu, in 1954. The Bulgarians, having lost two distinguished persons (Dimitrov and Kolarov) by death, were placed under the dominating figure of Chervenkov, who was not without intellectual and political capacity, and was party Secretary-General until 1954 and Prime Minister until 1956. The Rumanian leader, Gheorghiu-Dej, maintained complete control of the party from 1945 to the present and eliminated his rivals in successive purges. Chervenkov, on the other hand, soon after the death of Stalin, lost some of his power, and his position as party Secretary, to Zhivkov; the latter is much more a party *apparatchik* than a veteran revolutionary, and like Gheorghiu-Dej, a home communist, in contrast to Chervenkov, a long-time resident of the Soviet Union.

The death of Stalin and the beginning of de-Stalinization brought similar repercussions, but with each country presenting its own national variant. In neither case did the secret speech by Khrushchev produce the ferment, intellectual and political, that it did in Hungary or Poland. Changes in policy were minimal in both countries, and consisted, apart from the superficial changing of street names and removing of monuments, of some economic concessions, and certain reforms in agricultural and industrial management, in the administration of justice, and in local government, resembling those of the Soviet Union. In Bulgaria the political effects were much more striking, with the beginning of an assault on Chervenkov for the "cult of personality" which he had allegedly introduced into the party and into Bulgarian life generally. There was not a shadow of criticism of his illustrious predecessor, Dimitrov. Of significance in the process of de-Stalinization was the admission that the trial of Kostov had been based on fraudulent evidence. Chervenkov, already removed from the party secretaryship, lost the premiership but retained his membership in the Politburo, and continued to exercise considerable power. Some resistance to official policy, apparently expressing itself in a demand for more extreme measures of de-Stalinization, occurred, as was revealed later with the removal of Chankov, Terpeshev, and Panov from the top ranks in July, 1957. Among Bulgarian writers, however, the new course in Soviet Russia produced at the end of 1957 a lively intellectual ferment, which went beyond the realm of literature and touched on sensitive issues of party policy. It was finally brought under control by Chervenkov himself, from his new position as Minister of Education and Culture. A virulent campaign against revisionism ensued, embracing not only Bulgarian offenders, but also Yugoslav, and even Polish, deviationists. In 1959 and 1961 new oppositions occurred in connection with the Bulgarian "leap forward," but these were minor and easily settled by dismissal of the offenders.

In Rumania there was similar resistance among the top leaders to the official course, and, it would seem, demands for a more far-reaching revision of policies. Again this was laid bare only in mid-1957, with the removal of Chisinevski and Constantinescu from the leadership. Among intellectuals, there was nothing in any way comparable to the "revolt" in Bulgaria, and no serious "revisionism" manifested itself. Nonetheless the Rumanians dutifully launched a campaign against revisionism, chiefly in its Yugoslav form, but this lacked the bitterness and the fury of its Bulgarian counterpart. Gheorghiu-Dej was able to ward off any detrimental personal consequences of the attack on Stalinism, and indeed sought to avoid a large-scale assault on the "cult of personality" in its Rumanian form. To the extent that it had existed, it was blamed on former deviationists, such as Pauker and Luca, and was said to have already been largely overcome even before Khrushchev's speech in 1956. Even in Bulgaria, it might be added, the seriousness of Stalinism was denied, Stalin himself was more than once defended, and Chervenkov was said to have been of very different stuff than the Hungarian, Rákosi. In sum, in both Bulgaria and Rumania, the difficulties occasioned by the secret speech, and still more by the Hungarian and Polish events in 1956, were brought under control by the régimes, and Stalinism, under a new name, and in the case of Bulgaria, under a new leader, was maintained in large measure intact.

When the renewed attack on Stalin and Stalinism occurred at the XXII Congress in 1961, the political repercussions were much deeper in Bulgaria than in Rumania. In the latter, the cutting edge of the anti-Stalin campaign, this time much more vigorous than after 1956, was turned against the previously expelled leaders, including not only Pauker and Luca, but also, ironically enough, Chisinevski and Constantinescu, previously accused of "misinterpreting" the XX Congress decisions. Gheorghiu-Dej was praised in an increasingly adulatory manner as the wise leader who had averted the worst effects of Stalinism in Rumania. His position had been greatly strengthened, not only by the elimination of his rivals, but by his elevation to the position of Head of State after the constitutional revision and the formation of a State Council in early 1961. The visit of Khrushchev to Rumania in the summer of 1962 constituted a triumphant endorsement of the leader who had survived all changes in Soviet policy and who, for political longevity, was rivalled only by Hoxha in Albania and Ulbricht in East Germany.

In the case of Bulgaria, the main effect of the XXII Congress was to make Chervenkov the chief target and scapegoat for all the evils of Stalinism, which were said to have extended into every facet of life, economic and cultural as well as political. Chervenkov was finally eliminated from all positions and removed from the Politburo. A persistent campaign against him and the cult of personality suggested that the supporters of the former leader, and his ideas and practices, had by no means been overcome. In March, 1962, extensive government changes were made, the most notable of which was the removal of G. Tsankov, Minister of the Interior since 1950, and his Deputy Minister, Kolchev, and of General Mihailov, Minister of Defence.

Discussions among writers in early 1962 revealed great unrest and much mutual suspicion and hostility between former Stalinist authors and cultural officials, and their critics. The continued attention to cultural and ideological matters, including the visit of the Soviet chief ideologist, Ilichev, in April, suggested widespread uncertainty and disaffection among Bulgarian intellectuals and ideologues. The visit of Khrushchev in May, with its public endorsement of the Zhivkov leadership, was no doubt intended to buttress it against the continuing influence of Chervenkov and his supporters. The Zhivkov régime was thus given the additional strength needed to meet increasing economic difficulties, but could not boast of the political stability of its Rumanian neighbour.

As far as inter-bloc relations are concerned, the position of Bulgaria and Rumania have not seriously differed. The Soviet Union could rely on both for full support in all its difficulties, especially with Yugoslavia, China, and Albania, and found them orthodox and loyal supporters at successive world communist conferences. This is not to deny significant nuances of difference, especially noticeable in the case of Bulgaria. At first somewhat fascinated by the Chinese "leap forward" and the communes in 1958, the Bulgarians, much under the influence of Chervenkov and his visit to China at that time, took their own leap forward and even toyed with the idea of "communes," only to drop them quickly. There is no evidence that Bulgaria at any time considered siding with remote China against its historic Russian associate and close neighbour, or that in the later ideological dispute Bulgaria gave any aid or comfort to the Chinese. It can only be speculated that Chervenkov was not very sympathetic to the Khrushchev 1961 line with regard to Stalinism, of which he was the chief victim, and may harbour considerable sympathy for Albanian and Chinese criticism of Khrushchev's revisionism. Yugoslavia was also a potential source of Bulgarian suspicion of the Khrushchev line, as ideological differences were reinforced, as we have seen, by long-standing territorial conflicts over Macedonia. Again it can only be speculated that the new course of friendship with Yugoslavia might well have occasioned concern among present Bulgarian leaders and provided another motive for the Khrushchev visit.

Rumania had provided the forum, at its party congress in 1960, for a full-scale confrontation of Soviet-Chinese opinions but could hardly be suspected of anything but unconditional support for the Soviet viewpoint. Rumania had evinced no sympathy for the Chinese "leap forward," and indeed had publicly prided herself on achieving considerable economic results by slow and gradual development, without "leaps." Nor was Rumania averse to *rapprochement* with Yugoslavia, as she had been from the first slow, and continued lukewarm, in the campaign against Titoist revisionism. Having no important territorial conflict with Yugoslavia, Bucharest has been for some years conducting bilateral negotiations with Belgrade, Bulgaria deliberately and unwillingly excluded, concerning joint power developments on the Danube at the Iron Gate. Once again, in spite of many factors that might have suggested the contrary, Rumania showed herself to be somewhat more reliable than her Balkan neighbour from the standpoint of the Kremlin and its present rulers.

It would be impossible within the scope of this report to examine in any fullness the course of economic development in the two neighbouring satellites. Both countries have, needless to say, sought to revolutionize the backward economies inherited from the past, and have in fact transformed the face of the land and city. The nationalization of trade and industry was accomplished early. Successive long-range plans promoted industrial growth at a breakneck speed, averaging, for instance, a 16 per cent annual increase in industrial production between 1947 and 1958 in Bulgaria. Although the corresponding rate was somewhat slower in Rumania, the five year plan beginning in 1960 projected an annual increase of 13 per cent, a rate which was actually exceeded, it is claimed, in the first two years of the plan's execution. In 1959 Bulgaria's "great leap" forward seemed to have produced continuing rapid industrial growth, but to have failed to achieve its grandiose objectives, especially in agriculture. Since then Bulgaria has reverted to more reasonable targets in both industry and agriculture. In agriculture Bulgaria was the first country, after the Soviet Union, to complete collectivization, in 1958, and proceeded to follow Soviet policies in the merging of collectives, the abolition of compulsory deliveries, and the purchase of the Machine Tractor Stations. Rumania, after a relatively slow start, put on a hectic burst of speed in 1961–62, and reached the target of complete collectivization forecast for 1965. On the other hand, so far, Rumania seems not to have merged the collectives, or transferred to them the machinery of the M.T.S.

Both countries now consider that they have achieved the "building of socialism" and will no doubt register this, as did Czechoslovakia, in new "socialist" constitutions. This had been publicly forecast in Rumania, but a similar prediction in Bulgaria in 1961 seems to have been nullified by the XXII Congress and the subsequent heralding of a new constitution in the U.S.S.R. Whatever "socialism" may actually mean, the transformation of both countries from predominantly agricultural lands of small peasants into mixed agricultural-industrial economies, with industry and trade entirely nationalized, and agriculture totally collectivized, has not eliminated difficulties or solved all economic problems. Indeed the continued emphasis on industrial development, especially heavy industry, has slowed down the rate of agricultural growth and delayed a large improvement in the standard of living, so that the masses of both countries remain poorly clothed, poorly housed, and to some degree poorly fed. Rumania, with an area and a population twice as large as Bulgaria, and a much greater wealth of resources, seems to have been able to mould an economy that is more successful and prosperous than that of its smaller ally. Rumanian collectivization, it is claimed, was achieved without a decline in production, and without the grave shortages plaguing other Eastern European satellites. In Bulgaria, the effects of collectivization and lack of machinery, aggravated by several bad crop years, have produced a state of serious crisis, in sharp contrast to the relatively flourishing condition of the Rumanian economy. In view of this and the political difficulties described earlier, it is perhaps not surprising that the Bulgarian party congress, scheduled for August, 1962, was postponed until November.

Apart from the more successful management of her socialized economy, Rumania also seems to have distinguished herself by a somewhat greater originality in the working out of the forms of industrial and agricultural administration. On the whole, the Bulgarian administrative system has followed sedulously Soviet forms. Rumania, on the other hand, has been slower in adopting the measures introduced by Khrushchev at home. Her relatively small-scale industrial system did not suffer so much from the evils of over-centralism, so that reorganization on the Soviet model was not so urgent. Industry is for the most part still operated by central ministries, and local regional economic councils, established in 1961, have a purely advisory and controlling function. Rumania became the first country of the Soviet bloc to abolish her Ministry of Agriculture, replacing it with a large Agricultural Council, made up of agronomists, specialists, farm managers, and so forth, and competent to supervise and, in effect, direct the whole of agriculture through the medium of regional and district agricultural councils of similar composition. A similar effort to enlist mass participation and to make central management somewhat more collective was evident in the replacement of the Ministry of Education and Culture by a Ministry of Education, and a Committee on Culture, with regional and district cultural committees. This does not, of course, eliminate central control, and ultimate direction of all fields by the party, but seems to indicate a greater freshness in working out a Rumanian pattern of institutions.

Conclusions must be somewhat mixed and tentative. In spite of long-standing historical and cultural reasons for close relations with the Soviet Union, Bulgaria shows more evidence of potential disaffection—the historic conflict with Yugoslavia, continuing Chervenkov influence, and perhaps lingering sympathy with China. These seem at the moment more than balanced by the very dependence of Zhivkov on Soviet support in view of serious economic difficulties and political instability. Rumania, on the other hand, in spite of historical factors pointing in the opposite direction, evinces much less reason for conflict with Soviet Russia and its present course. Yet its relative political stability, economic success, and absence of serious intellectual ferment, strengthen its position *vis-à-vis* the U.S.S.R. and reinforce the tendency observed to do things in the Rumanian way. In the last analysis, however, Gheorghiu-Dej seems as dependent on Soviet support as Zhivkov, and shows no more overt sign of dissatisfaction with current Soviet policies. Both seem little worried by the Albanian defection and not in the least inclined to support China against Russia.

In the meantime there is much to be done. Their economies already closely integrated with the Soviet Union and the bloc through Comecon, Bulgaria and Rumania have accepted the latest decisions of that organization at its Moscow conference in 1962 to speed up the process of co-ordinating the Soviet and the satellite economies, thereby strengthening the bloc politically and helping its individual members meet the growing threat of the European Common Market.[1] A hardly less important objective of Comecon's strategy of unification is to equalize the economic level of all its members and thus to prepare the way for the gradual, and more or less simultaneous, transition of the "socialist" countries to the higher stage of communism. To the degree that these latter goals are achieved,

[1]Almost simultaneously with the writing of this article, Rumania began to show signs of resisting the bloc's economic integration and subsequently demonstrated increasing unwillingness to accept Soviet policy in this respect. See final chapter.

the freedom of manoeuvre of the bloc members in political as well as economic respects will be more than ever limited, and the uniformity of their institutions and of their life generally will be intensified. Until that "happy" day, if it is *ever* reached, the differentiation of bloc members, such as Bulgaria and Rumania, based on many historical and contemporary factors, and their relative autonomy of action in the post-Stalin "commonwealth" of socialist nations, make any serious prediction of their future difficult, if not impossible. The Albanian case should have warned us anew of the danger of prophecy in this most uncertain of political worlds.

5

TWO EX-SATELLITES *

ALBANIA AND YUGOSLAVIA together present one of the most
striking and baffling paradoxes of the communist world. These
close neighbours on the Adriatic shore of the Balkan peninsula
are both communist states, and have gone through political
experiences not unlike each other. Yet their relationship has
been for years one of almost unrelieved hostility which shows
no sign of abating. Both régimes were established at about the
same time, in the closing years of World War II, and by the
somewhat similar historical process of partisan action, with
little or no direct military aid from the Soviet Union. Indeed,
Albania owes much to the assistance of Yugoslavia at that
time, in the forming both of her partisan movement and of the
Communist party itself, and in the economic development of
the country in the first years after liberation. Both have shown
a similar unwillingness to accept certain Soviet policies or to
consent to Soviet dictation, and a common ability to defend
their independence successfully against Soviet pressure, the
Yugoslavs since 1948, the Albanians since 1961. Both may,
therefore, be regarded as ex-satellites, their membership in the
communist bloc and in its institutions having terminated.
Strangely enough, these common experiences have not brought
them together. Even the Albanian breach with the Soviet
Union, which bears striking resemblances to that of Yugoslavia fifteen years earlier, has not produced any noticeable
change of attitude of the two states towards each other. Nor

*Published in *International Journal*, XVIII, No. 3 (Summer, 1963).

has there been as yet any substantial modification of Albanian institutions or practices which would suggest an approximation to the "path towards socialism" which Yugoslavia has been gradually evolving these past fifteen years.

At the time of their expulsion from the Soviet bloc there was a sharp contrast in the position and the role of the two countries. In 1948, Yugoslavia, a substantial state of 15,000,000 people, enjoyed a special status in the communist world as one of the most loyal of satellites, enjoying much favour as the seat of the Cominform and its newspaper, *For a Lasting Peace, For a People's Democracy!* Its ruling party had been forged by the Comintern as an instrument of Soviet policy, and its leader, Tito, an old Muscovite, had been placed in command by Moscow in 1937. At a time when other "people's democracies" were proclaiming their own national path to socialism and in some cases the communists were sharing power with other parties, the Communist party of Yugoslavia was supreme and was following a full-blown "socialist course." In 1961, Albania, a tiny country of only 1,600,000 people (with almost a million of its co-nationals living in southern Yugoslavia), could play only a minor role in the communist world system. At first a "satellite of a satellite" (namely, Yugoslavia), heavily dependent on the latter for its economic support, from 1948 on it had replaced Belgrade with Moscow as its chief external support. A member of both the Warsaw alliance and Comecon, Albania was peripheral to both, and hardly a member capable of exerting profound influence. Its ruling party, formed only in 1941, and under Yugoslav rather than Soviet patronage, had had no connection with the Comintern and only nominal association with the Cominform. Its leader, Enver Hoxha, had had little or no direct experience with Moscow and was a home-grown product, who, however, during Stalin's lifetime and in the first years of Khrushchev's leadership, had demonstrated exemplary loyalty and devotion to Moscow and faithful emulation of Soviet policies at home and abroad.

The procedure by which Albania was driven out of the bloc in 1961 and became an ex-satellite was strikingly reminiscent of the process of Yugoslavia's expulsion.[1] In each case the initiative came, not from the expelled, but from the expeller, with the Soviet Union unilaterally denouncing the heretic after a period of secret negotiations, without extensive consultation with other Communist parties. The final public condemnation of Yugoslavia took place formally at a meeting of the Cominform, when the other European Communist parties associated themselves with the edict from Moscow. In the case of Albania, the formal act of expulsion was performed by Khrushchev himself at a meeting of the Soviet party, the XXII Congress, although the other parties had been aware of the growing estrangement of the Albanian and Soviet parties at communist gatherings in Bucharest and Moscow in 1960. It was left for the delegates to the C.P.S.U. Congress from the fraternal parties, and for their parties' subsequent Central Committee meetings, to indicate their solidarity, or lack of it, with the Soviet action. In both cases the final breach had been preceded by bitter ideological and political controversy, behind closed doors or in secret correspondence, and by various forms of Soviet pressure, such as the withdrawal of specialists from the smaller countries, and the ejection of their students from the U.S.S.R.

The break was followed by even more severe sanctions, in the shape of a savage campaign of ideological denunciation, the withdrawal of diplomats, and the interruption of trade relations. In the case of Albania, the other European communist states maintained some measure of diplomatic relations and renewed trade treaties with Albania during 1962, although the U.S.S.R. itself completely severed both diplomatic and economic associations. In both cases, there were not too thinly veiled appeals by Soviet leaders to the people of the party members of the condemned countries to overthrow their régimes or replace their leaders with others, but in each case without any response. In neither case was the U.S.S.R. willing, or able, to employ military methods to bring the dissident states into line, the geographic isolation of both Yugoslavia

[1]See William E. Griffith, *Albania and the Sino-Soviet Dispute* (Cambridge, Mass., 1963).

and Albania constituting an important ingredient in their safety from Soviet military action. Both Yugoslavia and Albania professed a willingness to engage in negotiations with the Soviet leadership in an effort to settle the dispute, and even in multilateral discussions with the other bloc members, but only on the basis of a complete equality of status with the others, a condition which in their own opinion was not adequately satisfied. In the case of Albania, the methods of pressure and of expulsion were essentially the same as those used by Stalin, and were equally ineffective in breaking the will and the ability to resist of the condemned state. The striking uniqueness of the Albanian case was that she was not alone, but enjoyed the support of China in her conflict with the U.S.S.R.

An ironic aspect of similarity between the early phase of the Yugoslav and the Albanian expulsions was the attitude taken towards the initiator of the break. For Yugoslavia, her ejection was unexpected, and unjustified, inasmuch as her loyalty to the U.S.S.R. was, in her view, unsullied and her policies not as divergent as charged. Even her faith in Stalin was at first undiminished. Professions of innocence, assertions of continued loyalty, and appeals for discussion and unbiased investigations, were ingredients of her defence.[2] Even after Stalin had shown himself unrelenting and had become the chief target of Yugoslav attack, her continued friendship with the Soviet Union and belief in Marxism and Leninism were proclaimed. The Albanians offered another variant of this attitude of injured innocence. No bones were made of their serious differences with Soviet policy, and of their bitter hostility to Khrushchev.[3] Like the Yugoslavs, the Albanians were convinced of their own rightness and of their political orthodoxy, and proclaimed their undeviating loyalty to the 1957 and 1960 proclamations of world communism. A campaign began at once, however, against the Soviet leader, Khrushchev, as the personification of revisionism and a betrayer of the common political line adopted at the Moscow conferences. Like the

[2]See *The Soviet-Yugoslav Dispute* (London and New York, 1948).
[3]Hoxha's speech of Nov. 7, 1961.

Yugoslavs, however, they never ceased to asseverate their eternal love for the Soviet Union and the C.P.S.U., and their belief in Marxism-Leninism.[4] Nor did they abandon their belief in the necessity of absolute unity in the ranks of world communism, and their claim to remain a member of the camp and its organs, the Warsaw alliance and Comecon.

A central issue in the two cases was the question of power, or control of the country concerned and its ultimate fate. Titoism has been explained as a vindication of Tito's claim to exercise full and independent control of the Yugoslav Communist party and the Yugoslav régime, and as a successful challenge to Stalin's efforts to retain and extend his own domination of Yugoslavia.[5] In a similar sense the breach between Albania and the U.S.S.R. was a conflict for power, a struggle between Khrushchev and Hoxha for dominion in Albania. In both cases, the personal fortunes of Hoxha and Tito, and their closest associates, were at stake, since victory for the Soviet Union would have involved the removal of the top leaders from their supreme position.

The two local masters differed widely in their personal history. Hoxha, a man of education, indeed the only topmost European communist leader with a higher education, had been converted to communism during his student days in France, and had only a remote tie with the U.S.S.R. as an object of theoretical affection and loyalty. Quite unlike the factory worker, Tito, whose communist education had been in the Moscow offices of the Comintern, Hoxha shared with Tito, however, the wartime partisan experience and the feeling that communism had been won in their land by their own efforts, with little or no Soviet aid. In both cases the leadership of the condemned party presented a strong united front against external pressure, and no serious defections in favour of the Soviet Union occurred. In the case of Yugoslavia, the loyalty of Tito's associates had been forged in the bitter school of the wartime resistance movement, and the party had not experienced any post-war feuds or purges. Only two of the top lead-

[4]Hoxha's speech of May 30, 1962.
[5]Adam Ulam, *Titoism and the Cominform* (Cambridge, Mass., 1952).

ers, A. Hebrang, and S. Zhujović, showed signs of pro-Soviet feeling and were removed without difficulty. The unity of the Hoxha leadership was of a different character, having been moulded by successive post-war purges, eliminating leaders deemed to be pro-Yugoslav (Koci Xoxe, 1948; Tuk Jakova and Bedri Spahiu, 1954; Liri Gega and others, 1956) and those considered pro-Soviet (Liri Belishova and Koco Tashko, 1961). Hoxha's supremacy was, therefore, much more Stalinist in type, based on terror and purge, as well as on family and tribal associations which bound many of the topmost leaders together. It was, nonetheless, a leading corps just as difficult to permeate from the outside as that of Tito, so that no disunity manifested itself in the comparable time of crisis.

Much more than a struggle for power and leadership was involved, however. In each case there was a fundamental and serious difference of view over communist policy and strategy, which in large measure generated the conflict and was intensified as it proceeded. In the case of Yugoslavia, the divergences were at first veiled and indistinct, and only gradually crystallized into full and open conflict after the breach had occurred. In the Albanian case, the cleavage was deep and obvious before the rupture and was the main factor in precipitating it. Indeed the Albanian case cannot be understood apart from the Sino-Soviet dispute, which began to develop after the death of Stalin and reached an acute stage in 1960 and 1961.[6] Although Albanian sympathy for Chinese views and distaste for the Soviet had been emerging since 1955 and 1956, it took on increasingly serious dimensions as the Sino-Soviet dispute sharpened. Particularly in the summer and fall of 1960, Albania became more and more involved in conflict with the U.S.S.R., and an Albanian-Chinese alliance gradually evolved. Albania thus played the part of a tiny sympathizer and supporter of its distant and giant friend, and not of an entirely independent actor as did Yugoslavia in 1948. In her continuing struggle with the Soviet Union, the Albanians are buoyed up by the thought that "we are not alone," a theme often repeated

[6]See Griffith, *Albania and the Sino-Soviet Dispute,* and Donald Zagoria, *The Sino-Soviet Conflict 1956–1961* (Princeton, 1962).

during 1961 and 1962. Yugoslavia had at first no such anchor to leeward, and although it had some supporters in other parties in Eastern Europe, these were soon crushed by Stalin and his local supporters.

It is impossible to discuss here the fundamental disagreements between China and the Soviet Union which have developed during the decade since Stalin's death. These touch on basic issues of domestic policy; questions of foreign policy, such as peaceful coexistence, disarmament, nuclear weapons, and foreign aid; the strategy of revolution in non-communist lands; leadership and unity within the socialist camp; the attitude to be taken towards Yugoslavia, and so forth. Although the discussion has been in ideological terms, it is beyond doubt that deep questions of policy are involved, and indeed openly expressed in rival interpretations of doctrine. For a long time, the target of the Chinese was Titoist Yugoslavia, bitterly attacked ever since 1948 by the Albanians; the targets of the Soviet Union were at first unnamed "dogmatists" and from 1961, the Albanians. But behind these immediate targets stood the chief protagonists, China and the U.S.S.R., for whom the smaller countries were mere stand-ins or substitutes in the hidden debate. When open polemics were later resorted to, the association of Albania and China, and of the Soviet Union and Yugoslavia, was clearly revealed.

The Chinese (and the Albanians) have been expounding views regarded by Moscow as "leftist" or "dogmatist," and the Soviet Russians (and the Yugoslavs), views regarded by Peking as "rightist" or "revisionist." Although these terms often distort and becloud the points at issue, to some degree they are useful terms of analysis, and bring out an important difference between the experiences of 1948 and 1961. Yugoslavia, which had, prior to its break, occupied a position somewhat "leftist" as compared with its fellow communist states, increasingly came to take a place on the extreme "right" of the spectrum of communist interpretation of doctrine and policy. In an opposite manner, China, which had been "rightist" in its support of Poland and Hungary at the early stage of the thaw period, moved sharply to the left in 1958, and became increas-

ingly radical in its view of the world and in its interpretation
of the common doctrine. Meanwhile the shifting of Soviet
policy towards a "centrist" position more acceptable to Tito
has bridged some of the gap between Yugoslavia and the
U.S.S.R., and has opened up a gulf on the other side between
the U.S.S.R. and communists of more leftist persuasion in
China, Albania, and elsewhere. At the earlier world conferences, China and the Soviet Union were able to agree that, of
the two dangers facing their movement, the greatest was
"rightism" or "revisionism" as represented by Yugoslavia. Later,
however, with the gradual shift of positions, and the sharpening conflict of China and the U.S.S.R., the latter openly suggested that the greatest danger lay on the "left."[7]

At the present time, on all matters of policy, ideology, and
strategy, Albania stands squarely and firmly in the Chinese
camp. Her ideological pronouncements endorse all the major
Chinese positions on the nature of imperialism, the possibility
of peaceful coexistence, the course of future revolution, and
leadership of the communist camp. Like China, Albania considers herself a correct interpreter and follower of Marx and
Lenin, and indeed of Stalin, and openly denounces Khrushchev as an arch revisionist, close to Tito in his attitudes on
domestic and world policies. China has repeatedly paid tribute to the correct Marxist-Leninist position of the Albanian
Workers' party, and has published its statements in full in the
Chinese press. While bitterly criticizing Khrushchev's analysis
of imperialism and his belief in the possibility of coexistence,
and condemning specific courses taken by the Soviet Union
in the Cuban and the Sino-Indian crises, Albania has, nonetheless, continued to espouse, with the Chinese, the notion of a
unified monolithic communist bloc, and even the idea of
Soviet leadership. But it is clear that she wishes to see the bloc
led by some person other than Khrushchev, and in another
direction than that chosen by him and approved by the majority of communist states and parties. Even more a *bête noire*
is Yugoslavia, regarded as an exponent of a contemporary

---

[7]See Khrushchev's speech to the Supreme Soviet, during Tito's visit,
Izvestiya, Dec. 13, 1962.

Bernstein revisionism and as an agency of world imperialism. In other words, the Albanians, like the Chinese, persist in the view of Yugoslavia set forth by the Cominform in 1948 at the time of the expulsion.[8] In 1955–56, Albania publicly endorsed the Soviet *rapprochement* wth Yugoslavia, but without enthusiasm, and rejected any rehabilitation of Xoxe. When the campaign against Yugoslavia was resumed in late 1956, Albania was among the most virulent in her abuse of Tito and in particular of Tito's role in the Hungarian revolution. There can be little doubt that the renewed efforts by the U.S.S.R. to resume somewhat more friendly relations with Yugoslavia was one of the major reasons for Albania's fear and distrust of Soviet policy.[9]

Yugoslavia's position, in matters of policy and ideology, is in most ways directly opposed to that of Albania. Like the latter, however, she regards herself as following a correct Marxist, and even Leninist, path, but rejects Stalinist "distortions" of the fundamental doctrine and consciously seeks to revise and adapt it to the needs of the contemporary world and her own national conditions. Indeed this viewpoint, expressed most systematically in the programme of the League of Yugoslav Communists in 1958, brought down upon her head the fires of denunciation, not only of the Albanians and the Chinese, but of the rest of the communist world, including Soviet Russia. Although the Soviet campaign has been much toned down after years of bitter condemnation, important ideological differences still remain between Yugoslavia and the Soviet Union and its supporters. They continue to regard her as a revisionist state and particularly criticize her failure to associate with the bloc, and the military alliance of the Warsaw Pact. Her evaluation of world imperialism, of capitalism, and of future revolution, and her attitude to communist unity and leadership are, however, much more moderate and balanced than that of the extremists of Peking and Tirana, and much closer to that of Moscow. Khrushchev has increasingly

[8]See for instance Hoxha's speech of Nov. 7, 1961.
[9]See Griffith, *Albania and the Sino-Soviet Dispute*, pp. 156–7, and *Zeri i Popullit*, June 30 and Sept. 19, 20, 1962.

chosen to minimize the differences in his deliberate reconciliation with Yugoslavia as a state, but the more dogmatic ideolo-
gists of Peking and Tirana continue to regard the Yugoslav
deviation as an insuperable obstacle to any *rapprochement*.

In foreign policy matters, the positions of Yugoslavia and
Albania are curiously opposed. Whereas Yugoslavia still rejects
membership in the Soviet bloc, and indeed the very idea of a
bloc approach to world affairs, Albania still adheres to a kind
of old-fashioned "two-world" concept, with a united communist camp seen as the only safeguard against the threat of
American imperialism. Although expelled from the Warsaw
alliance and from Comecon, she considers herself, strangely
enough, a member of the communist system and criticizes her
exclusion from these bodies. On the other hand, Yugoslavia
continues to find herself on the same side as the U.S.S.R. on
basic questions of foreign affairs, such as disarmament, nuclear tests, the Sino-Indian border conflict, the Caribbean
crisis, and the Berlin question, whereas Albania has shown
herself steadily more critical of Soviet foreign policy on all
these matters. At the same time Yugoslavia persists in her
course of "independence" or "non-alignment" in world affairs,
and strives to maintain friendly relations with the United
States and other states. In the years since the open break,
Albania has shown little or no evidence of a shift towards
greater friendliness to the West, especially to the U.S., such
as occurred in the case of Yugoslavia after 1948. Albania has
not adopted a neutralist position, nor a pro-American stance,
and remains "aligned," but with China rather than with the
U.S.S.R. Even in questions of relations within the communist
world, Albania's concept of a unified and monolithic camp
under Soviet leadership is directly opposed to Yugoslavia's
notion of a polycentric system in which all communist states
and parties retain complete independence and a status of
equality.

Institutionally, substantive differences exist between the two
communist states. In Yugoslavia, as is well known, after an
initial period of uncertainty, there occurred, in the years since
1950, gradual changes in industrial management, the planning

system, agricultural tenure, the role of the party, and intellectual life, thus giving substantial content to the idea of a national path to socialism distinct from that of the Soviet Union. A new constitution adopted in 1962 embodies many of these special features of Yugoslav communism. Albania, on the contrary, remains largely unchanged, even since the death of Stalin. There have been no basic alterations in institutions and procedures comparable to those that have occurred in the Soviet Union, still less to the shifts in Poland and Hungary. Perhaps, given time, an "Albanian way" might emerge, as a Yugoslav did, but at present there is no sign of even the germs of such an evolution. Albanian industrial administration remains highly centralized, without even that degree of reorganization carried through in the Soviet Union, whereas Yugoslavia, in spite of a deliberate trend towards greater central control in the past twelve months, retains much of her distinctive system of workers' management and local autonomy. Agriculture continues to be completely collectivized in Albania, since its completion in 1959, whereas Yugoslav agriculture is not more than 20 per cent collective and shows no sign of an impending drive towards greater collectivization. In intellectual life, Albania, like a kind of European Tibet, remains isolated from the outside world, including even the communist countries other than China since the interruption of cultural exchanges with the bloc. In Yugoslavia, although there is not the atmosphere of relative freedom in scholarship and the creative arts of Poland, there is a good deal of rational research, a lively artistic experimentation, and extensive cultural relations with the West, and to a limited degree with the Soviet Union, and with Poland. In these and other respects, it is clear that Albania remains the conservative, and Yugoslavia the liberal, in terms of freedom, experimentation, and reform of the basic institutions inherited from the period of Stalinist conformism.

Khrushchev's campaign of de-Stalinization introduced another somewhat confusing issue on which again the positions of Albania and Yugoslavia were sharply opposed. For Yugoslavs, Stalin had come to be regarded as the main culprit in the Soviet mistreatment of their country, and as the chief target of their resistance. The adoption by Khrushchev of a policy of de-Stalinization at the XX Congress in 1956, was greeted by Yugoslavs as the turning of a new leaf both within the U.S.S.R. and in relations with other communist countries. Yugoslavia has tended to sympathize with Khrushchev's course and to regard him as the main bulwark against a restoration of Stalinism. Their interpretation of Soviet politics has assumed a continuing struggle within the Soviet Union and other bloc countries between unrepentant Stalinists, such as Molotov, or Chervenkov, or Hoxha, and the progressive forces seeking to carry through a more thorough reform of the system. In this light, the renewed assault on Stalin by Khrushchev in 1961 was considered a necessary further step in this struggle. The attack on Albania, although strikingly similar in method to the Stalin assault on Yugoslavia in 1948, was, therefore, also welcomed, as was any sign of removal of Stalinist methods and elements from other neighbouring communist countries.

At home, the personal pre-eminence of Tito, and the substantial cult of his personality, are reminiscent of Stalinism, but his position is much more that of a first among equals within the leading corps, and as a result of his wartime record and his defiance of Moscow, a broadly based national role of leadership. Moreover, in spite of the treatment of Djilas, there is not the ubiquity of terror characteristic of full-blown Stalinism. Nor has Yugoslavia been reluctant to dismantle many of the institutions and procedures inherited from the Stalin period, and to revise essential theoretical aspects of Stalinism as a doctrine. As in Khrushchev's Russia, there are continuing features of communism not unlike those of Stalin's system, but a substantial measure of reform has indeed been carried through.

At the opposite pole stand China and Albania. China is not in any genuine sense more Stalinist than Yugoslavia or the Soviet Union, nor can her leftist policies be regarded as essentially Stalinist. There is, however, substantial evidence of Chinese dissatisfaction, from 1956 on, with Khrushchev's de-Stalinization campaign, in the main because it was launched without prior consultation with China and other partners, and because it brought damaging consequences to the world communist movement and even threatened the stability of certain communist régimes.[10] Albania at first evinced no open dissatisfaction with Khrushchev's action, and indeed verbally associated itself with the general line of de-Stalinization.[11] Pressure at home for more energetic measures in this direction in 1955 and 1956 was rejected, and only minimal steps were taken. The role of Hoxha as supreme dictator and the cult of his person was not seriously modified, and there has been no purge of Stalinist elements from high places. After the break with Moscow, Hoxha avowed his disagreement with the line of the XX Congress, and accused Khrushchev of using charges of Stalinism as instruments of pressure and propaganda against Albania.[12] Beginning with 1960, Albania began publicly to restore the image of Stalin, dilating on his positive achievements and waxing more and more fulsome in praise of Stalinism.[13] Little information is available as to the degree of popular support and the unity of the Albanian leadership. Soviet treatment of Albania has no doubt tended to knit together the leadership and the people in a national unity comparable to that produced in Yugoslavia in 1948. Any serious measures of de-Stalinization, however, would threaten the position of the present leaders, if not the very existence of the régime.

It has often been argued that, in spite of ideological and political appearances, the essence of the Soviet-Yugoslav and the Soviet-Albanian disputes has been nationalism—the determination of a small nation to assert its independence against a domineering great power. Even the Soviet Union has explained (and equated) the attitudes of Albania and Yugoslavia towards her in terms of excessive nationalism. In each case national pride and confidence have been reinforced by their

[10]Zagoria, *The Sino-Soviet Conflict 1956–1961*, Chapter I.

[11]Hoxha's speech at the Congress of the Albanian Workers' party, in May, 1956.

[12]See Hoxha's speech of Nov. 7, 1961.

[13]See in particular the editorial in *Zeri i Popullit*, Dec. 21, 1961; cf. Hoxha's defence of Stalin at the Central Committee, Feb. 13, 1957.

experience in World War II in establishing communism by their own efforts, with a minimum of aid from the Soviet Union, and by their success in maintaining their independence since the breach. There can be little doubt that in the case of Yugoslavia, the fact that they have been able to weather fifteen years of repeated assaults from the Soviet Union and have indeed compelled Khrushchev more than once to admit defeat, has intensified, not only their fear and suspicion of the U.S.S.R., but also their own feeling of self-confidence. This achievement has tended to moderate national and religious hostilities at home and to weld the Yugoslavs into a single nation, and has had the parallel effect of solidifying the relations of régime and people and making Tito something of a national hero. Traditional fears of their neighbours, and territorial conflicts with Bulgaria, Albania, Hungary, and Greece, have introduced a further nationalist element into the struggle with the Soviet Union and its supporters, aggravating the ideological hostility of Yugoslavia and her Balkan communist neighbours.

Nationalism has expressed itself somewhat differently, but nonetheless potently, in the Albanian break with the Soviet Union. Like Yugoslavia, the national struggle for independence is still relatively fresh in the memories of Albanians, culminating in independence, on paper, only in 1912, and in reality, as late as 1920. This liberation was achieved, and later maintained, only at the cost of bitter conflict with all of its neighbours, Yugoslavia, Greece, and Italy, so that Albania has suffered from what has been called an "encirclement complex."[14] As already noted, Albanian fortunes as a communist land were, at first, linked closely with Yugoslavia, her initial patron. In spite of this, or perhaps because of this, Albania swung to the Soviet side in 1948, and sought in the U.S.S.R. a balance against her closest neighbour to the north. In subsequent years, there was no louder voice in the anti-Yugoslav communist chorus than Tirana's, and *rapprochements* between Yugoslavia and the U.S.S.R. brought only modest, and reluctant,

[14]See Wolfgang Höpker, "Albanien—Europas 'verbotenes Land,'" *Osteuropa*, VIII, No. 4 (April, 1958), p. 234.

modification of Albanian attacks. Although this hostility was in part ideological, there seems little doubt that it was in large part a nationalist reaction, based on traditional fear of her northern neighbour and suspicion of her territorial designs.[15] This fear is intensified by the existence of a strong Albanian (or Shiptar) minority in southern Yugoslavia, in the Kosmet autonomous region. Although these Shiptars enjoy wide cultural rights and modest home rule, this area is regarded by Albanians as a region of cultural oppression, and as a zone of irredentism directed against the very integrity of Albania. Nor is it surprising that Albania herself has aspirations towards the ultimate incorporation of these Shiptars in her own small population. As long as the Soviet Union and its partners were engaged in bitter ideological denunciation of Yugoslavia, traditional Albanian hatred of Yugoslavia did not introduce a jarring note. The more recent effort of both the Soviet Union and Yugoslavia to achieve a reconciliation in the political sphere was bound to conflict with Albania's nationalism, and to arouse new fears of a possible Soviet assignment of Albania to Yugoslavia as a sphere of influence or zone of expansion.[16] Apart from political and ideological sympathies which Albania entertained for the Chinese, she saw in China a balancing power that could be used to protect her own independence against both Yugoslavia and the U.S.S.R.

The experience of Yugoslavia and Albania illustrate anew the enormous potential of national communism and the ever changing nature of the world communist system. Soviet "control" of her "satellites" is by no means as absolute as this term has normally suggested. If two satellites, such as Yugoslavia and Albania, can with impunity become ex-satellites, the usefulness of the term is itself brought into question. Political satellites, like earth satellites, are no longer doomed to eternal movement in a predestined orbit, but may now take their fate

[15]See for instance Griffith, *Albania and the Sino-Soviet Dispute*, p. 174; also J. F. Brown, "Albania, Mirror of Conflict," *Survey*, No. 40 (Jan., 1962), pp. 24–41.

[16]See Djilas' revelations of earlier Soviet approval of Yugoslav plans for amalgamating Albania and Yugoslavia: Milovan Djilas, *Conversations with Stalin* (London, 1962), pp. 120–33, 154–64.

in their own hands, and, like manned *sputniki*, determine their course independently of the launching point. Other dissidents, such as Hungary and Poland, were less successful in vindicating their claims to independence, but have, by their actions in 1956, made their own contribution to the loosening of the ties of the self-styled "commonwealth of socialist nations." This, and similar events in the future, may lead to the ultimate fragmentation of the communist system into separate and competing blocs, especially now that China and Soviet Russia stand as rival points of attraction for other communist states and parties. Individual communist countries may choose to associate with one or other of the great powers of the communist world on a voluntary basis, as Albania has done with China, and Yugoslavia, to a degree, with the U.S.S.R. Although settlement of the Sino-Soviet conflict through mutual compromise does not now seem likely, neither of the two ex-satellites, in such an event, would be willing to return to a community of communist nations which did not recognize their equality of status and assure them a substantial measure of genuine autonomy.

6

STALIN OVER PRAGUE *

THE ENORMOUS STATUE of Stalin, which, until October, 1962, overlooked ancient Prague from its commanding position above the Vltava, seemed to symbolize the continuing "orthodoxy" of a communist country that had changed but little since the death of Stalin. True, the demolition of this huge group of stone figures was physically not as easy as that of its smaller counterpart in Budapest, which was torn down in a matter of hours in 1956. But even the smaller statue in Bratislava, which could easily have been removed, gazed down benevolently on the May Day procession in 1962 as it passed through Stalin Square. In fact, in the year which followed the XXII Congress in October, 1961, Czechoslovakia, unlike some of its neighbours, was hardly influenced at all by the new spirit of Moscow, and showed no signs of relaxing its strongly Stalinist course. Paradoxically, this country, almost unique in its devotion and subservience to Moscow, was increasingly out of step with Khrushchev's policy of de-Stalinization. "Orthodoxy" seemed to be evolving into "heterodoxy."

Ever since the Prague coup in 1948, indeed, Czechoslovakia had usually been regarded in the West as the "loyal" or "stable" satellite, offering no spark of resistance to the general line of the U.S.S.R., showing no serious signs of intellectual or political ferment, and weathering the crisis of the post-Stalin thaw without significant changes of leadership or policy. Even during the critical months of 1956, Czechoslovakia had re-

*Published in part in *The Economist*, June 2, 1962, and in *Canadian Slavonic Papers*, VI, 1964.

mained a model of Stalinist orthodoxy, and exhibited few symptoms of the "fever" which had infected other satellites, notably her closest neighbours to north and south. What little unrest manifested itself was easily dampened down by the régime, so that the Poles and Hungarians in October found no support from Czechs or Slovaks. From the communist viewpoint, Czechoslovakia was a most faithful associate of the Soviet Union, showing no evidence of dangerous disaffection or domestic instability, and giving her full support to the Moscow gospel as interpreted by Khrushchev. Indeed, with the proclaimed completion of socialism in 1960 and the embodiment of this "fact" in the new constitution of that year, the Czechs and Slovaks seemed to stand in the van of the communist camp, their country being the only member which, like the Soviet Union, had finished the building of socialism, and was standing on the threshold of full communism.[1] The fact that it had failed to follow Khrushchev under the banner of de-Stalinization seemed to have been forgiven in the light of its otherwise impeccable loyalty and domestic stability.

Why was Czechoslovak communism so submissive to Moscow, and yet so Stalinist, so slow to change? These questions, often posed in Prague, brought a variety of responses. Official communist replies dwelt on the "positive" factors which had contributed to this imperviousness to change. For one thing, the roots of Czech communism (although not of the Slovak branch) were much deeper than those of Hungarian or Polish, extending back into a strong Social Democratic movement in the Bohemian and Moravian lands of pre-1914 Austria, and expressing itself in substantial electoral strength of Czech communism between the world wars. Indeed during and after World War II, and even earlier, at the time of Munich, Czech communism was able to identify itself with strong currents of public opinion and to create an image of itself as a powerful and progressive movement deserving support. In 1945, when the Czech communists stood on the threshold of power, unlike

[1]See H. Gordon Skilling, "The Czechoslovak Constitution of 1960 and the Transition to Communism," *The Journal of Politics*, XXIV, No. 1 (February, 1962).

their comrades in Budapest or Bucharest, or even in Warsaw, they formed a movement, which, although decimated by wartime losses, possessed a strong cadre of leaders and members, capable of rapid expansion to form a massive party. Hostility to communism, of course, also existed in some quarters, but it was countered by a widespread sympathetic view of the Soviet Union as a friendly Slavic power, and of communism as a progressive social force. It was possible, therefore, for substantial non-communist parties, and leaders such as Eduard Beneš and Jan Masaryk, to envisage a policy of close collaboration with the communists in the post-war republic, and with the U.S.S.R. as a reliable ally against the German menace.

Czechoslovak nationalism, moreover, had historically been somewhat milder and less fantical than that of its immediate neighbours, and had not involved the historic hostility towards Russia characteristic of both Hungary and Poland. Less heroic and romantic in cast, Czech nationalism had not prevented co-operation with foreign rulers such as the Hapsburgs. There had indeed been a long national tradition of accepting and adapting to alien authority, even while bringing it into contempt, represented in the literary figure of "the good soldier, Svejk." After 1945 there were no Soviet troops in Czechoslovakia to serve as a daily reminder of foreign domination and to generate burning national hatred. In any case, the historic enemy had been, not Russia, as in the case of Hungary, or Russia *and* Germany, as in the case of Poland, but Germany alone. The attitude towards this hereditary enemy was less impassioned than that of the Poles, but enough had been suffered, especially during the war, to push the Czechs and the Slovaks to the Soviet side of world affairs. The alliance with the Soviet Union was, therefore, in large measure a matter of the national interest, and not merely a question of communist ideological sympathies.

For these and other reasons, the transition to power was easier than elsewhere, and occurred without the necessity of widespread violence. Indeed, in 1948, the strategic and tactical skill of the communist leaders, who were able to establish a monopoly of power without bloodshed, and indeed without significant resistance, had paralysed the opposition of anti-communist forces, and generated a certain enthusiasm for the new order among the communist rank and file. Czech communists, once in power, were heirs to valuable assets not present elsewhere in communist Europe: a highly industrialized economy, an efficient agriculture, a competent and incorrupt civil service, an experienced managerial class, and a skilled, well-organized, and numerically large working class. All of these factors served as the basis of a relatively advanced and productive economic system, and at least for a time, a relatively high standard of living. The régime was, therefore, able to proceed with a much wider public consensus to a drastic reorientation of the economy, the planned reorganization of industry and agriculture, and even the political and cultural assimilation of the whole of society to communist patterns. It was not compelled, to the same degree as in Hungary or Poland, to impose everything from above, against the will of the overwhelming majority.

There were other more "negative" factors, acknowledged by disillusioned or dissident party members, as well as by non-communists, which influenced the style of Czechoslovak communism. From 1929 onward, Czech and Slovak communist leaders had with few exceptions been utterly devoted in their obedience to the Soviet party. Entirely uninfluenced themselves by Czechoslovak democratic traditions, these leaders, headed by Klement Gottwald, made their régime a model of Stalinism, and a pillar of strength for communism in Eastern Europe. Western traditions, and the national traditions of Masaryk and Beneš, were submerged under the flood of the complete Stalinization of all aspects of national life. In politics, the economy, in law and in culture, the emulation of all things Soviet was accepted as the fundamental of party and government policy, and the gradual approximation of Czechoslovak life to Soviet patterns was the proclaimed target. In Slovakia, where communism had much less appeal for a devoutly Catholic and largely peasant people, and where nationalism had been promoted by the short-lived German-sponsored "independence" during the war, the policy of the Communist party of Czechoslovakia (C.P.C.) after 1947 subordinated the Slovaks to increasingly centralist rule from Prague, and trod underfoot the nationalist feelings even of Slovak communists. Even the personal cult of Stalin was duplicated in that of Gottwald, culminating after his death in the embalming of his body for public display in a manner adopted outside the U.S.S.R. only in the case of the Bulgarian, Dimitrov.

Apart from this grotesque manifestation of Byzantinism in a profoundly Western country, the course followed was little different to that of her fellow satellites, who all rejected, after 1948, the notion of "a national path towards socialism" and embarked on the "Soviet" or "Leninist" course. The system of terror was no less severe than in Albania, Hungary, and Bulgaria, and in some respects went even further than these classic practitioners of this art. As in these three countries, political show trials culminated in the execution of top party leaders, an experience avoided by the Poles, and even the East Germans. In addition to the main trial of Rudolf Slánský and his thirteen associates in 1952, there was a whole series of similar trials, some of them occurring as late as 1954, after the death of Stalin. Slánský was not particularly popular, so that his execution did not produce the revulsion occasioned by the similar treatment of a Kostov, or a Rajk. Other victims were highly respected and intelligent leaders, whose execution or imprisonment severely shook the morale of communist cadres at all levels. The anti-semitic element of the Slánský trial, and the noticeably anti-Slovak character of the execution of Vladimir Clementis and the imprisonment of other Slovak leaders, such as Laco Novomeský and Gustav Husák, contributed to the decline of faith of the ordinary party member, but as far as is known, did not produce a single act of protest by a leading figure of the communist movement.

In the ten years since Stalin's death, the most striking feature of Czechoslovak communism has been its failure to modify the essential features of the system as it had been created under Stalin and Gottwald. The early post-1953 thaw was minimal, expressing itself mainly in a carefully controlled "new course" in the economy that did not break radically with the past and

was easily reversed again somewhat later. It involved in the
main a greater accent on consumers' goods production and a
slowing down of collectivization. The riots in Pilsen in 1953,
created by the monetary reforms, did not reflect such widespread disaffection as the almost simultaneous uprising in
Berlin, or the later disturbances in Poznań, and were easily
put under control, without much violence. The death of
Gottwald immediately after Stalin's demise made unnecessary
drastic changes of leadership such as occurred in Hungary.
His successor as President, Antonín Zápotocký, was peculiarly
appropriate for the period as he was a distinguished trade
union and party veteran, whose personal career extended back
to Austrian and Czech Social Democracy before 1914, and
who had won a certain respect and popularity even among
non-communists. Real power, however, no doubt rested in the
hands of the new party chief, Antonín Novotný, an entirely
colourless *apparatchik* who succeeded Gottwald as General
Secretary in 1953, and who assumed the office of the presidency on Zápotocký's death in 1957. A "faceless" person, lacking any popularity, Novotný was a product of the Gottwald
party apparatus, and was clearly not destined to be the spokesman of a liberal or national communism. Later events were to
show that he lacked the independent will and strong character
of a Tito or Gomułka, or even the pragmatic originality of a
Kádár, and was much more a counterpart of the Bulgarian
apparatchik, Zhivkov.

Indeed, there were no conditions in Czechoslovakia comparable to those of Poland and Hungary, still less of Albania
or Yugoslavia, which would have led the country on to the
path of national communism. Apart from Gottwald's death,
and the removal in 1956 of his son-in-law, Alexei Cepička,
Minister of National Defence, from this post and from the
party leadership, there were almost no changes in the top
command. The party was still run by the same corps of Gottwald associates who had been by his side during the entire
post-war period, some of them since 1929—Karol Bacílek,
Jaromír Dolanský, Václav Kopecký, Viliam Siroký, and Zdeněk
Fierlinger, augmented by products of the party apparatus who

had attained to high rank either at the time of the Slánský trial, such as Novotný, or later in the post-Stalin period, such as Rudolf Barák, Pavol David, and Jiří Hendrych, and a few technical specialists, such as Oto Simůnek. All the key figures, including Novotný, had been directly and deeply involved in the Stalinist system, and therefore personally feared any serious effort at de-Stalinization. The party command did not seem to be divided into rival and competing wings such as played an important role in paving the way for October in Hungary. "Liberal" spokesmen there were none, except perhaps Zápotocký, who, it is reported, attempted to speed up the process of rehabilitation after the XX Congress, but without success. The completeness of Stalinist terror had brought about a situation where there was no one capable of giving leadership to a new anti-Stalinist course after 1956. Slánský was dead, and in any case would hardly have been a likely candidate for leadership of a liberal or national communism. The charges of Titoism which had formed part of his original indictment were no doubt in the main falsified, as was officially admitted in 1956. Other more liberal persons, such as Clementis, had also been executed, so that there was no Gomułka or Kádár who might emerge from confinement to give leadership to progressive forces. Nor was there a Tito or Hoxha, or any similar leader determined to resist unwelcome Soviet pressure. Czech and Slovak communist leaders were too closely bound and too subservient to the Soviet Union to act independently, too fearful of their own position to give expression to public disaffection. Nor is there any evidence to suggest that Moscow was pressing them hard to de-Stalinize, being evidently willing to tolerate a Stalinist system which was loyal rather than to run the risk of instability by pressing for serious changes. After 1956, there was even less reason to urge the Czech leaders to take the dangerous course of reform which had helped to produce the catastrophe in Hungary.

Nor was there strong popular pressure from below, as in the case of Poland and Hungary, where this had combined with intervention from Moscow and dissidence among the top leaders to produce the crises of 1956. There was discontent, but it was given little or no opportunity to express itself or to influence the course of events. The Czech leaders did not make the "mistake" of their Hungarian colleagues of permitting widespread criticism of Stalinism and the existing state of affairs. Above all, there was no intellectual unrest such as sparked the ultimate political crises in Warsaw and Budapest. The Stalinist system had created an atmosphere of fear which persisted long after Stalin's death, rendering difficult and dangerous a revival of criticism and discussion. There was some literary ferment in April, 1956, especially at the Second Writers' Congress, but as in Bulgaria and Rumania, it was brought under control at once at the party conference in June, so that it was not a factor at the time of the October crises. The cultural policy of Zdeněk Nejedlý, Václav Kopecký, and Ladislav Stoll had produced complete sterility in Czech and Slovak Marxism, and had made most intellectuals obedient servants of doctrinal orthodoxy, so that there was no one capable of stimulating a reassessment of Marxism, and generating a movement towards revisionism, as in Poland and Hungary. The Hungarian crisis had created some hopes of change, but was an enervating and frightening experience, intensifying feelings of guilt among Czechs and Slovaks, who remained largely passive during these stirring events.

The picture of Czechoslovakia as the entirely silent and passive satellite is, however, usually overdrawn, and neglects the imponderables of human psychology. In some respects the shattering effect of Stalinism had been far worse in Czechoslovakia than elsewhere since the democratic tradition had been more deeply rooted than in other countries of Eastern Europe. Even after the war, for several years, there had been a substantial restoration of freedom in the period of coalition under Beneš. The Czechoslovak democratic tradition had been in the main parliamentary rather than revolutionary, and had therefore not been well suited either to compete with communist strategy in 1948 or to deal with communist power afterwards. The successive discouragements of 1938 and 1948, and even of 1945, had no doubt weakened the morale of the Czechs and dulled their will to resist. Nonetheless the traditions of

Masaryk and Beneš had had a profound influence on the thinking of the people as a whole, including some communists, so
that the régime had, prior to 1953, resorted to a vicious campaign to discredit both Masaryk and Beneš and to eliminate
the "vestiges" of their ideas from the minds of the people. This
was later replaced by a kind of silent treatment of these great
figures of Czechoslovak history. The persistent affection for
them among the ordinary Czechs, if not Slovaks, was no doubt
a factor which discouraged the communists from making meaningful concessions in the direction of greater freedom.

Although the leaders complimented themselves on the absence of an organized system of "revisionist" thought prior to
1956, they admitted that during the 1956 days there had been
proposals for an emergency party congress and a change in the
party line, and other evidence of "wrong thinking." Some people,
it was lamented, had utilized the campaign against Stalinism
as an occasion for attacking Marxism-Leninism itself, and the
general line of the party. Even after 1956, there were frequent
official references to the dangers of bourgeois and "revisionist"
ideas, suggesting that these were tenacious and substantial
"vestiges" which were regarded as a continuing danger.[2]

After 1956 it was easy and natural for the Czechoslovak
leaders to swing back into the old channels, feeling that they
had done well to avoid the excessive thaw of Hungary and
Poland, and had been confirmed in their slowness in de-
Stalinization. Indeed the Soviet Union, and especially Khrushchev, must have felt deeply appreciative of the steady course

[2]V. Koucký, a leading party ideologist, for instance, in an important
speech at a seminar devoted to the struggle against contemporary revisionism on October 16 and 17, 1958, complained of the demands for
"freedom and democracy in a bourgeois sense," and of vestiges of social
democratism, Masarykism, and nationalism," explaining it in terms of
the rapid growth of the party after 1948, and the pressure of bourgeois
ideology from outside (Rudé právo, Nov. 1). On the same occasion
Stoll explained this in terms of the fact that the communist régime had
taken over "a very numerous intelligentsia class which all too easily
succumbs to the political and ideological influence of the bourgeoisie,"
and thus created a "social ground" and "class psychological roots" for
hostile ideas (Ibid., Nov. 21, 1958). Both cited specific cases of this
in the press, in publishing, in philosophy, in the social sciences, and
among writers and students.

of Prague during and after that crisis, in particular the early
approval of the Soviet intervention in Hungary, and the full
support of the Moscow conference resolution at the end of
1957. The line of that conference, which depicted "revisionism"
as the main danger in the communist world, and dogmatism as
a less dangerous possibility, could not but appeal to a régime
that could hardly be called anything else but "dogmatist."
Nowhere in the bloc was the campaign against Yugoslav and
other forms of revisionism pressed with more energy and con-
sistency after the temporary interruption in 1956–57.[3] Even
when the emphasis began to shift in late 1960 and dogmatism
became more and more the target of attack, the Czechs continued for some time to condemn Yugoslav revisionism as well.
In this, as in all other matters of doctrine and foreign policy,
Czechoslovakia continued to show itself one of the most trust-
worthy supporters of Moscow. Novotný might well declare, on
July 2, 1958, during a visit to the U.S.S.R. that there "had
never been any divergence of views" between his and the
Soviet parties, and that "we shall always remain loyally by
your side."

Throughout the years after 1956 Novotný remained at the
helm, and there were no changes in the essentials of the political and economic system. The new constitution of 1960 was
intended to document the achievement of socialism, but did
not effect any appreciable alteration of the general structure of
power. Elections in that year were conducted in the old style.
There was much talk of democratization, but the role of the
non-communist parties remained unimportant, and there was
no real effort to enlist non-communist participation, as in the
case of Hungary. There were gestures in the direction of administrative decentralization, with the establishment of new
regional party and government organs, and with increased
competence for the national committees, changes which were
incorporated in the constitution of 1960. Although this dimin-
ished the excessive centralism of the old days, it did not
fundamentally alter the general scheme of centralized control
of public administration. As far as Slovakia was concerned, a

[3]See, for instance, *Rudé právo*, May 8, 1958.

modest broadening of the competence of Slovak organs in the 1956 days was reversed, and these organs were reduced to almost complete impotence in the new constitution. Even in the party the Slovaks were poorly represented at the centre, with their chief spokesman the Prime Minister, Siroký, and the Slovak party chief, Bacílek, both only partly Slovak in origin. Pavol David was the only undisputed Slovak in the party command. Lip-service was paid to the Leninist style of the party, expressed in the restoration of its democratic and collective aspects, but there was no real change in the concentration of power at the top. There was some improvement in legal procedures with the introduction of new criminal codes, and an amnesty of 1960 led to the release of thousands from imprisonment, including many who had suffered during the 1950's. However, a commission to re-examine the political trials, headed by the Minister of the Interior, Barák, produced no general revision of the trials or public rehabilitation of the victims. In the field of culture, these were years of increased emphasis on "party-mindedness" of literature and art, and of constant struggle against bourgeois ideas and revisionism, with the baton being passed back and forth between the hands of Kopecký, the Minister of Culture, and Stoll, who, following a temporary eclipse after 1956, again appeared in 1959 as one of the key arbiters of the party line in culture. Perhaps most striking of all was the continued bitter campaign against bourgeois nationalism in Slovakia, in which Bacílek played the leading role. Nor was there any effort to conciliate the churches, and Archbishop Beran of the Catholic Church remained in the confinement he had suffered since 1949.

After the XXII Congress of the C.P.S.U. in October, 1961, and the renewed attack by Khrushchev on the crimes of Stalin and the now discredited leaders of the anti-party bloc, the curious contradiction between Czechoslovakia's loyalty and doctrinal orthodoxy, and her failure to take any serious measures to end her Stalinist system became even more pronounced. The Czech and Slovak leaders verbally associated themselves with the renewed denunciation of Stalin and described it as a necessity in view of the tenacity of the opposition to Khrushchev's "new course." At the Central Committee in November, 1961, the Czechoslovak party accepted without reservation the measures taken by the C.P.S.U. Congress, and expressed its readiness to draw the appropriate conclusions for their own country. As Novotný, in his address, admitted, the "cult of personality" had made itself widely felt in Czechoslovakia too. There had been, he said, "some people" in the Czechoslovak party between 1948 and 1953 who had sought to impose their will on the party, who had abused their position of responsibility for their own advantage, and who had used the security organs for the suppression of criticism. The person mainly responsible for breaches of legality and for wrong party methods had been, he charged, the former General Secretary, Slánský, who had suffered the supreme penalty of death at the hands of the security machinery which he had himself built up. Even Gottwald was made to bear some of the blame. After his election to the presidency, it was alleged, he had become the subject of a cult of his own person, had ceased to keep in touch with the party from his presidential office, and had allowed Slánský to become the dominant force. This was in part due to the deterioration of Gottwald's health, of which Slánský had taken full advantage. Novotný did not, however, make a full frontal attack on the dead leader, as the Bulgarians were making on Chervenkov, or the Hungarians on Rákosi, and indeed declared that Gottwald's faults could not diminish the historic contribution that he had made to Czechoslovak communism. He remained "a great revolutionary fighter" and "the motive force of the whole party."

While shifting the main blame for Stalinism on to Slánský and the dead Gottwald, Novotný skillfully sought to deflect all responsibility from himself, noting at one point in his speech, "I was not in the innermost leadership of the party at that time," and at another point referring to the fact that he was "in contact" with Gottwald only in 1952. This was technically true only at the time of the Slánský arrest, in September, 1951, when Novotný held the office of Regional Party Secretary in Prague and was a member only of the Central Committee.

However, in that month, he replaced Slánský as a secretary of the Central Committee and in December, became a member of the political secretariat of the party. Novotný was thus a key figure before Gottwald's death, and then became General Secretary and bore major responsibility for the trials of Czech party officials and Slovak nationalists in 1954. Also conveniently ignored was his own important contribution to the case against Slánský, which was warmly and publicly praised in December, 1952 by Bacílek. Moreover, he also passed over in silence the fact that many who were still his closest associates, such as Kopecký, Siroký, and Bacílek, had been comrades of Gottwald during the whole of the Stalinist period; there was no suggestion that they bore any responsibility for the crimes of that era or should pay any penalty at this time. Nor was there any indication that any of Slánský's associates, or Slánský himself, were deserving of rehabilitation, posthumous or otherwise, although there was a vague reference to unnamed "innocent people" victimized during this period and restored to full party membership and at work again. Novotný rejected "irresponsible appeals to rehabilitate people" who were responsible for violations of legality, and rejected claims of some that they were "not guilty." "We do not see any reason," he declared, "why our party . . . should change its standpoints." Any remaining cases of violation of legality would be dealt with, he declared, but no one would be permitted to use "cases already settled" for "demagogic attacks against our party."

It was evident from Novotný's speech that the Czech leader wished to convey the impression that the worst period of Stalinism had ended with the execution of Slánský, and that after 1953, and again after 1956, the party had taken major steps to eliminate the cult of personality. Lip-service was paid to the need for proceeding further with the complete elimination of the consequences of the cult in all spheres of life, but few concrete indications were given as to what this in fact meant. Indeed Novotný confined himself to what might be termed "symbolic" de-Stalinization, such as the replacement of the Stalin statue, the removal of Gottwald's body from the mausoleum, and the completion of the renaming of streets called after Stalin or living communists. Although his speech implied that there was a widespread demand for a more thorough-going rehabilitation of those who had suffered during the Stalinist reign of terror, it was equally clear that he realized the dangerous potentialities of opening up this question more fully and proceeding to a full-scale public exoneration of all those victimized. There was no word of criticism of the political trials of 1951 and after, and no admission that they had been parodies of justice. The lessons of Hungary during the thaw period had not been lost upon Novotný; he was not going to permit his own position to be undermined, as Rákosi's had been, by a thorough revision of the crimes of the Stalin period.

In the year that followed between the Central Committee meeting and the twelfth congress of the C.P.C. in December, 1962, there were almost no significant changes for the better, and indeed some changes for the worse. For over six months a governmental committee wrestled with the embarrassing task of disposing of the Stalin statue. Only in August was their report published proposing its replacement by a building which would symbolize Czechoslovak-Soviet friendship and serve as a cultural and political centre for Prague. The actual demolition of the stone giant followed months later, in October. Only in late April was the name of Stalin Avenue in Prague quietly changed one night to one politically neutral, Vinohradská (Vineyard). At about the same time the mausoleum containing Gottwald's body on Vitkov Hill was closed for "technical reasons," but the re-interment of his ashes occurred only in October. Even more significantly, there had been little progress in the rehabilitation of those who had suffered legal injustice during the Stalin period.

In February, 1962, Rudolf Barák, a top-ranking member of the central leadership who had been a member of the Politburo from 1954, Minister of the Interior from September, 1953 to June, 1961, and a Deputy Prime Minister from 1959, was removed from all offices and excluded from the party. His trial in April, held in secret before a military tribunal, during which he is said to have admitted his guilt, led to a verdict of fifteen years in prison on the charge of abusing his position for personal economic gain. Other lesser officials of the Ministry of the Interior were also sentenced to shorter periods of imprisonment. Few took the charges of embezzlement seriously, and many thought that Novotný was thus settling accounts with a serious rival. Novotný had originally spoken of Barák's "personal political objectives, to be attained by the path of anti-party activity and by the creation of distrust in the organs of party and government."[4] The final verdict charged him only with economic crimes, but did refer to his "yearning for power" and called him "an intriguer and political adventurer." A relatively young man, forty-six years old, with a popular image of intelligence and ability, and a popularity not enjoyed by his other colleagues, Barák was regarded by many as the only member of the Politburo capable of providing leadership in a new, anti-Stalinist course.[5] True, he had been for long associated with the Novotný leadership, and was Minister of the Interior for many years, including the period of the later political trials. His career in high office had, however, been almost entirely in the period *after* Gottwald and Stalin. Most significantly, he had been chairman of the committee for re-examining the political trials, the report of which had not been published. Whether he had favoured swifter rehabilitation or more drastic de-Stalinization, or had uncovered evidence implicating some of his colleagues in high offices, is not known. It seems hard to believe

---

[4]*Rudé právo*, Feb. 23, 1962.

[5]A story circulating in Prague in the spring of 1962 was that Barák had sent a memorandum to Khrushchev professing his lack of agreement with Novotný's politics. Although there was no way of verifying or disproving this story, the fact that it was told and believed indicates the position occupied by Barák in the minds of some Czech communists. In a speech made at the time (April 12, 1962) but not published until a year later, Novotný admitted that some party organizations had expressed disagreement with the action taken against Barák. See *Usnesení a dokumenty ústředního výboru komunistické strany Československa od celostátní konference KSC 1960 do XII sjezdu KSC* (Prague, 1962), II, pp. 244–5.

that his relationship with the delicate and sensitive question of rehabilitation was not involved in the action against him.

The visitor to Prague at this time was impressed by the striking difference of atmosphere in comparison with that of Budapest, Warsaw, and Belgrade. There was a general air of caution and vagueness in official conversations, reflecting perhaps uncertainty about the future and discouragement concerning the present. There was much less knowledge of what was going on in the outside world, even in the Soviet Union, and a rather pathetic plea for information from the Western traveller. Apart from the exchange of specialists with bloc members and the movement of tourists to the Black Sea and other resorts, travel was severely circumscribed, so that Czechs and Slovaks, especially the younger ones, felt hemmed in within their narrow, centrally located country. As compared with the scholars of either Poland or Yugoslavia, communication with the outside world was limited; few cultural relations existed with the Western lands, or even with Eastern countries, other than Poland. There was no parallel to the limited freedom enjoyed at home by Polish or Yugoslav scholars, and a generally stifling pall seemed to hang over intellectual life. Ideology was at a low ebb. Marxism-Leninism was orthodox in the extreme and devoid of the limited creativity found in Poland, or even Hungary. There was no Czech Lukács, not even a Schaff, still less a Kołakowski. Students, although selected with due regard for "social origin" and "political reliability," did not find the official doctrine of Marxism-Leninism vital and meaningful. In ordinary life, fear still prevailed, said one expelled communist: "fear of the people by the régime, fear of the régime by the people, and fear of everyone for each other."

In the past, Czechoslovakia's relatively good economic situation had promoted the stability of a régime lacking wide public support. Now unexpected and unexplained economic difficulties had developed to plague the government. Long queues formed in the early morning outside every meat store in every village and town. Pork was in especially short supply, but beef was also scarce. In part this was due to the greatly increased meat consumption which was only partially met by the expansion in livestock production in 1961. In part it was due to the long winter, and the inadequate supplies of fodder. No doubt it reflected, too, the recently completed collectivization drive and the lack of incentives which farmers complained about. But the crisis had been accentuated by the interruption of normal trading relations with China and to a lesser extent, Albania, so that hard currency, which might have been used to cover emergency imports of meat and other scarce foodstuffs had been used for other more urgent supplies. Moreover the call-up of troops during the Berlin crisis, many of whom had still not been released, had accentuated the labour shortage in the countryside.

The hours of waiting in queues exasperated people who were already tired from long hours of work, "voluntary" brigades, and frequent political meetings. Not surprisingly, some Czechs talking to foreigners indulged in more uninhibited criticism than at earlier times. Gone was the enthusiasm of 1948, replaced by widespread disillusionment among many party members. Gloom and pessimism were everywhere to be found. Novotný found himself isolated, not only from the people at large, but also from wide sections of the party. His criticisms of his predecessor, Gottwald, and even more, of the respected Zápotocký, certainly did not endear this upstart to the older communists. The arrest and imprisonment of Rudolf Barák was bound to alienate his fellow post-war communist cadres.

There were few Czech or Slovak communists who entertained any special sympathy for Albania, or for China, or would have been willing lightly to endanger their close relations with the Soviet Union for the sake of either. All the same, the break with Albania and the conflict with China deeply unsettled them, and perhaps suggested to the leaders that a slow and cautious course at home was desirable until the final outcome of the Sino-Soviet conflict was known, and Khrushchev's victory over his domestic rivals indubitably confirmed.

While remaining largely passive in concrete action directed towards the de-Stalinization of Czechoslovak life, the party continued, however, to demonstrate its complete loyalty towards the Soviet Union on the broader international front. Vigorous criticism of revisionism continued, but was supplemented by bitter attacks on Albania and its so-called dogmatism. Indeed both revisionism and dogmatism were treated as equal dangers, and as of common origin, namely "nationalism"—"a position of national exclusiveness, betrayal of proletarian internationalism, the severance of fraternal bonds with the C.P.S.U. and the other Marxist parties."[6] The notion of the polycentrism of the international communist movement was rejected outright, and the "leading position" of the C.P.S.U., as "the only one centre,"[7] and as "the centre of creative Marxist-Leninist thinking"[8] was stressed.

In the light of later events it seems clear that there was considerable dissatisfaction, even among communists, with the snail's pace of de-Stalinization in Czechoslovakia.[9] There were even occasional voices raised publicly that "the condemnation of the cult of personality does not yet mean its complete destruction," that tearing down monuments and renaming streets was not enough, and that many "smaller cults" persisted and that "bureaucratic and arbitrary behaviour" continued. Party organs even admitted that "erroneous views" were expressed within the party, and that there were "people who would like best to blame the Central Committee itself for everything" and "to blacken honourable officials." This, it was said, must be absolutely rejected. The party was "not a debating society," and no one must be permitted "to abuse internal party democracy to the detriment of the party." The only criticism that could be tolerated was "party criticism," i.e. "that criticism which arises from the programme, the political

[6]*Nová mysl*, Dec. 12, 1961.

[7]J. Fojtík, *Rudé právo*, Dec. 12, 1961.

[8]*Rudé právo*, Feb. 14, 1962.

[9]In Novotný's speech of April 12, published one year later, he referred to resolutions of party organizations expressing lack of agreement with the C.P.C.'s attitude to the XXII Congress, representing the "voice of the class enemy," and manifesting "all kinds of incorrect opinions ranging from Social Democratism and opportunism through Trotzkyism and revisionism, to dogmatism" (*Usnesení a dokumenty*, II, pp. 244–5).

line of the party, and from the statutes and the decisions of the party."[10]

The twelfth congress of the Czechoslovak party, originally scheduled for October and finally held in December, was awaited with some expectancy, as the congresses of the sister parties in Sofia and Budapest in November had been significant stages in the process of de-Stalinizing these countries. The congress of the C.P.C., however, brought none of the spectacular purges of Stalinists of the Bulgarian party congress, nor did it, as the Hungarian party congress had done, confirm important leadership changes already made. In Czechoslovakia there was in fact only a minor re-shuffle in the leadership and the old guard seemed to be still safely in control. Although Novotný's position had no doubt been severely shaken by the economic crisis, he had been able to ward off any challenge such as may have been offered by Barák, and to avoid the risks that might have been engendered by a stricter course of de-Stalinization.[11]

The congress debate could not, however, avoid the latter question, and indeed once again suggested that there had been criticism of the speed of de-Stalinization, as well as some "surprise" on the part of those who were disturbed by the attacks on Gottwald and on Czech Stalinism. Both Novotný and his ideological lieutenant, Hendrych, expatiated on the evil effects of the cult of personality in Czechoslovakia in the past. Novotný went so far as to say that as a result, "the party had got itself into a position of isolation from the workers." Hendrych mounted a more drastic attack on Gottwald than previously, stating that the latter's activities after 1948 had been "entirely under the influence of the effects of the cult of personality." Indirectly replying to criticisms of de-Stalinization, Novotný referred to the elimination of the consequences of the cult as "not a matter of one decision or a single campaign," but "an uninterrupted process," implying that although there was still much to be done, the party was

[10]See the unsigned article in Zivot strany, No. 9 (May, 1962).
[11]For speeches at the Congress, see Rudé právo, Dec. 5, 1962, et seq.

systematically proceeding with the task. Hendrych admitted that the cult of personality was still present in Czechoslovakia and urged that all remnants of it must be rooted out. In a remark that perhaps sought to explain the failure to eliminate specific persons from their positions, and to diffuse the responsibility for Stalinist practices, Hendrych declared: "Each of us had in greater or lesser degree paid his due to the cult of personality." Novotný now admitted, for the first time, that most of the verdicts of the political trials of the fifties had been incorrect, although he announced that only thirty persons had been completely rehabilitated. Barák, he said, as chairman of the original committee of review, had protected certain culprits, and had suppressed some of the relevant information, hoping to use this in his own interest. All trials between 1949 and 1954, he announced, were to be again reviewed, with the whole matter to be finally cleared up within four months. Somewhat contradictorily, Hendrych declared that it was not necessary to change anything in the guilt of Slánský and certain other persons, thus clearly implying that certain limits had already been set to the ultimate effect of the reexamination.

A large part of the congress discussions was devoted to the grave economic crisis which had plagued the country throughout the year, and which had led to the decision, confirmed at the congress, to abandon the third five year plan and to replace it with a special plan for 1963, and a new seven year plan.[12] Far from seeking a solution in the liberalization of economic policy, however, the congress sought it in a reversal of the modest decentralization launched in 1958, and in a tightening up of the central control of the economy, both in industry, and agriculture, and in investment planning. Prime Minister Siroký, in his speech, dwelt almost exclusively on the serious consequences of "the weakening of central direction," and on the need for more stringent centralized

[12]Novotný in his unpublished speech of April 12, 1962, had dealt at length with the reasons for the crisis in the economy (*Usnesení a dokumenty*, II, pp. 224 ff.).

planning and administration. This was to be achieved by enhancing the responsibility of the government and the ministries, through the establishment of certain new central organs, such as a State Price Committee and an Agricultural Commission in the party's Central Committee, and of a new system of control organs, modelled on the Soviet pattern, extending throughout the country and responsible to a central agency. The revised party statutes, approved by the congress, were also designed primarily to "strengthen the leading role of the party" in the direction of the economy. There was certainly no evidence of an abandonment of the strictly centralist concept of economic management inherited from the days of Stalin and Gottwald.

The proceedings took place in an atmosphere of intensifying Soviet-Chinese conflict, and in a spirit of open Czechoslovak support for the Soviet position in this dispute. Although Czech leaders continued to speak of the danger of revisionism, there were friendly words for Yugoslavia, and the main target of attack was dogmatism, as represented by Albania. A number of speakers, including Novotný in his final statement, publicly rebuked the Chinese communists for their attitude towards Albania and made clear his full support of the Soviet line in foreign relations. Indeed, there were many glowing tributes to Soviet policy in general, and the C.P.S.U. programme, adopted at the XXII Congress, was openly proclaimed as "our own." There was also expressed the need to associate more and more closely with the Comecon plan for the international division of labour within the communist camp, and with the unified planning organs proposed by Khrushchev in this connection. This would lead ultimately, it was said, to a "unified economy" within the communist world, and indeed to the "gradual overcoming of differences" and an "approximation" of the individual communist countries. While, of course, these prognostications could hardly be meant to apply to China or Albania, they suggested the ever more intimate relationship that was envisaged for Czechoslovakia and the U.S.S.R.

Although nothing was predictable with certainty in the communist world, the situation in Prague following the congress at the end of 1962, suggested that the Czechoslovak régime had weathered the storm occasioned by the XXII Congress as well as its own internal difficulties, and had confirmed its reputation as the most stable but also the most static of the Eastern European satellites. A dramatic change in the scene seemed as little likely as that the Vltava would start flowing south to the Danube.

7

FERMENT AMONG CZECHS
AND SLOVAKS *

IN EARLY 1963, a fresh current of air began to be felt in Czechoslovakia, with more pungent and uninhibited criticism of
matters as far removed as literary criticism and economic planning. This modest liberalization of public discourse seemed
to reflect a mounting discontent beneath the surface with the
continued conformity of Czechoslovak political and cultural
life, but was not welcomed in high political circles.

In a speech delivered to the party *aktiv* in Ostrava at the
end of March, and devoted largely to the critical economic
situation, Novotný felt obliged to deal with broader questions
in a manner that was most revealing. Although he kept within
the framework of Khrushchev's recent statements as to the
inadmissibility of peaceful coexistence in the ideological
sphere, Novotný seemed to be speaking with peculiarly Czechoslovak circumstances in mind when he rejected any effort
"under a subjective view of freedom, to smuggle tendencies
of decadent capitalist society into our life, especially our culture." While avowing the need for "constructive" criticism, he
went on: "But to criticize everything, to make a fashion out
of it, to criticize socialist society, this we shall not permit. We
need criticism here as we need salt or our daily food, but no
one may touch our Communist party, its programme, or our
socialist order. This must be and must remain sacred for

*A briefer version published in *International Journal*, XIX, No. 4
(Autumn, 1964).

everyone." He proclaimed the right of the party "to direct cultural activity, just as it directs and leads the entire life of the country," and warned cultural and artistic workers that "they did not have a monopoly in criticism." They were not, he said, "special people differing from others," or " 'a God,' sent to this land so as to judge the people's life from their exalted position like a conscience, and on the basis of this human activity, to reach god-like conclusions." Reverting to more directly political matters, Novotný declared that they were going to "finish with" the cult of personality, but this did not mean, "under the shield of the struggle against the cult of personality, to attack what the working class, led by the Communist party, had struggled for decades to achieve, and to smuggle into our life bourgeois liberalism."[1]

Jan Fojtík, an ideological spokesman for the party, reiterated this theme a few days later in an important article on "the cult of personality and the way to overcome it."[2] He deplored what he called "a one-sided emotional approach in its evaluation" and "a certain mistrust in face of the removal of its vestiges," which had resulted from "the immorality and indeed criminality" involved in the phenomenon. He rejected the view that it was better to "overshoot in criticism, rather than overlook anything," and argued that this attitude "overlooked the actual efforts of the party, even before the XX Congress in some respects, to settle accounts with the past of the cult." Then, in a manner reminiscent of Novotný, he sought to walk the same tight-rope, balancing between the need for freedom, and the necessity to limit it. Strongly stating the desirability of "a free exchange of opinions," he also warned that this did not mean "rotten liberalism." People should not be tyrannized for their views; no one should claim "absolute correctness"; and "logic" should not be "replaced by arguments based on position." This did not mean, he went on, that "everyone will have his own saint," and it must not be allowed to endanger the authority of the party, and its right to criticize opinions and to forbid attacks on the foundations

[1] *Rudé právo*, March 24, 1963.
[2] *Ibid.*, March 29, 1963.

of the system. This did not represent, he asserted, a return to the practices of the period of the cult.

An even more revelatory indication of the tenseness of the situation was given in the leading article in *Nová mysl* by its editor-in-chief, Cestmír Císař, entitled "The Pure Shield of Communism."[3] Arguing that a great deal had been accomplished since the XX Congress in 1956, he admitted that much remained to be done. "Every marking of time means a loss of momentum and the prolongation of an unsatisfactory situation." Re-stating the familiar theme that the liquidation of the cult of personality was not easy and was a "continuing process," he said:

The cult of personality was not a simple ideological matter involving the adoration of a leading person; it was a whole system of views, customs, organizational measures, procedures and methods, which were deeply rooted in life and stubbornly persist.[4] It must also not be overlooked that it is the same people who struggle with the remnants of the cult of personality who used to be for many years subect to it and who got used to its norms and methods; it was said at the Congress that everyone of us has paid his due to that era and everyone of us has made a larger or smaller contribution. To rid oneself of deep-rooted ideas and habits requires a hard struggle within oneself and around oneself, a struggle of truthful recognition against false illusions, a struggle of party honour against petty vanity, a struggle of daring innovations against comfortable conservatism.

In this struggle, which may be characterized as a great process of discovery, some will understand the meaning of the revival of Leninism more quickly, others more slowly; some will adapt themselves superficially, others will experience a profound transformation; some cannot wait to see new conditions everywhere corresponding to the course embarked upon; others counsel cautious waiting.

Like other spokesmen, Císař proclaimed the leading role of the party in this process and declared that "it will not allow any one else to claim to be the nation's conscience and to push

[3]No. 4, April, 1963, pp. 385–97.
[4]At another point, he wrote: "The search for 'hidden enemies' had created an asphyxiating atmosphere of general suspicion within the party, of distrust between comrade and comrade, which spread also outside the party in relations with non-party people. This had a serious demoralizing effect on the masses of communists."

the party to the side-lines."[5] At another point, he repeated that "we shall not allow any one to take advantage of the complicated and difficult struggle of our party for his own anti-popular purposes." At the same time he made the rather surprising admission, not only that the party had made serious mistakes, but that its decisions even then were characterized by the "relativity of truth." The party, he said, should itself be made the object of scientific study, under the guidance of the Central Committee, so as to "distinguish the positive and negative sides of party work" and "the effectiveness of the forms and methods by which its leading role is carried out."

Then, in a comment that was directed generally to leaders of the party at all levels, Císař made the rather remarkable statement:

No wonder that the conservative elements in the party are losing the confidence of the communists and the non-communists alike, and are losing their former authority. It is a tragedy when they do not understand this in time and cling tooth and nail to functions and positions once gained. This is harmful for the party and its good name among the masses. And it is not beneficial, when party organs look on passively.

Communists were only human, he noted, and continued:

One understands when any man, who was once appreciated and raised above others by the collective, and who has a certain degree of ambition, easily begins to exaggerate his own merits and capacities, uncritically becomes the victim of subjective notions and views, and disregards the opinions of the collective of his comrades. When he remains for a lengthy period in a position once attained, is not criticized for his errors, and is permitted excesses distorting party policy, he may easily get on to the slippery slope so well-known from the days of the cult of personality.

Even more strikingly, referring to persons raised to leading positions in the past, Císař spoke of "some" who "have stagnated at the level once attained, keep on relying on their

[5] In a speech at the Congress of Czechoslovak Journalists, Císař rejected the idea of "absolute freedom of the press or anarchy of opinion" and defended the party's right to intervene "against errors." This should not be regarded as "an attack on one's right to express freely one's own opinion or any return to the administrative measures of the past, or an effort at silencing" (*Rudé právo*, April 23, 1963).

former merits, do not improve their qualifications, continue to commit greater errors in their work and harm the sector entrusted to them. There is no doubt that they must be replaced." These words were, of course, not necessarily directed at Novotný and his colleagues at the top, but might easily have been so intended, or so interpreted by readers of these lines in the party organ.

It was difficult to know whether Císař was acting as a spokesman of the party leadership, or of its critics, in these somewhat cryptic but explosive remarks. On April 4, almost at the time of the publication of this editorial, and certainly in its spirit, there occurred an event unparallelled in the recent history of Czechoslovak communism, namely, the removal from office of two outstanding party veterans, Karol Bacílek and Bruno Köhler, both founding members of the C.P.C., leading party activists before World War II, and prominent in central organs throughout most of the post-war years. The waves of de-Stalinization were beginning to touch for the first time the topmost level of the Czech party. This drastic action was announced publicly only six weeks later, on May 14. A few days before the announcement, Novotný somewhat pathetically soliloquized about the hazards of leadership, stating in a speech on May 9, that "people come and go, but the party is eternal." Although he was seeking to shift the blame for past mistakes onto his two former colleagues, his position could hardly fail to be shaken by their removal.

Bacílek, a Politburo member since 1951, had been Minister of State Control (1951–52) and of National Security (1952–1953) at the peak of the terror, and had been top party boss in Slovakia from 1953 ever since the purge of the prominent Slovak "nationalists." At the time of his own removal, he was First Secretary of the Slovak party, as well as a member of the central party Presidium. Köhler, less prominent publicly after the war due to his German nationality, had nonetheless held high posts in the central party apparatus during the Slánský trials, and had been a Central Committee secretary since 1953. Until the congress of the party in December, 1952, he had also been a candidate member of the Presidium. He was now deprived of his seat on the secretariat. A lesser figure, Václav Slávík, by profession a journalist, who had after 1956 been a Central Committee *apparatchik*, and after 1961 a secretary of the Central Committee, was also dropped. Bacílek's place on the Presidium and as First Secretary of the Slovak party was taken by Alexander Dubček, who had emerged among the top ranks in the period after 1958. Of the two new secretaries, the most significant was Cestmír Císař, who, although not previously even a member of the Central Committee, had been chief editor of *Nová mysl*. The other newcomer, František Penc, had been an industrial administrator and like Císař, had occupied leading posts only in recent years. In June, the Slovak party excluded from its Presidium not only Bacílek, but also Pavol David, a member since 1954, and since 1952 a Slovak Central Committee secretary.

At the time of the fall from grace of Bacílek and Köhler, a lengthy editorial in *Rudé právo*[6] revealed that the Central Committee had also devoted its meeting to the question of rehabilitation and that the General Procurator had submitted to the Supreme Court proposals for the "civil and legal rehabilitation of leading party and state functionaries who had been unjustly condemned in the political trials in the years 1949 to 1954." Evidently the announcement had been long and carefully prepared within the ranks of the party. It had been the subject of discussions in all party organizations in the weeks following the Central Committee, it was said, and had received overwhelming approval. Party membership would be restored to all who were shown to be guiltless, but denied to those who had broken party principles. "The working people of our country can today have the firm certainty that the negative phenomena of the period of the cult of personality belong irretrievably to the past," read the editorial. "This step is at the same time our contribution to the strengthening of the ideological and action unity of the international communist movement in its struggle for the triumph of peace and socialism." The editorial returned to the oft-repeated theme that everyone must be conscious of his own

[6]May 14, 1963.

share in the incorrect methods and errors of the past, and must not content himself with referring to "the errors of others." This would strengthen "the authority of the whole party." In an appeal for the restoration of Leninist principles of action, such as party unity, collective leadership, criticism, and self-criticism, the editorial called for "comradely relations among all its members, rectitude in action, openness in criticism, objectivity and principledness in decision-making, receptivity and attention to the needs of the people."

There were, no doubt, many communists who felt that the concern of their leaders for "the authority of the party" was much more a concern for the security of their own position, and that they were seeking to diffuse their own responsibility for past actions within a guilt which they claimed was shared by all. An editorial by M. Hysko in the Slovak party organ, *Pravda*, suggested that this familiar argument was not accepted by many party members. The writer agreed that the C.P.C. as a whole might be absolved from responsibility, because the rank and file had been excluded from decisions, the views of the chief head had been treated as "immutable dogma," and members were supposed passively to accept ready-made and unchangeable decisions handed down from above. From this thesis, which itself might have been acceptable to the party bosses (although not if it implied that a similar situation continued to exist), Hysko drew the unorthodox conclusion that it was "not the whole party and all communists alike" who were responsible but "primarily concrete persons," especially "those who after the XX Congress of the C.P.S.U. impeded the efforts of the party for a consistent implementation of the Congress decisions."[7]

These events, and others yet to be described, suggested that at long last the log-jam of Czechoslovak orthodoxy was beginning to break. An earlier hint of change had been the quiet removal in March, for "reasons of health," of Josef

[7]May 8, 1963. In an earlier article in *Pravda* (March 28) Hysko had roundly declared that half measures were not enough in eliminating the consequences of the personality cult and clearly suggested that those who had suffered injustice deserved to be publicly rehabilitated.

Urválek, Chief Prosecutor in the Slánský trial, from the position of Chairman of the Supreme Court which he had occupied ever since 1953. On May 1 student demonstrations took place at the statue of the poet, Karel Hynek Mácha. What official propaganda called anti-African manifestations by so-called "hooligans" occurred in Prague streets in the subsequent two weeks. Although the content of the report on the trials was not yet publicly known, party members no doubt had some prior knowledge of it and were beginning to sense that important events were impending. Even before the announcement of the fate of Bacílek and Köhler, indignation was being sharply expressed at the Congress of Slovak Writers, held from April 22, in Bratislava, and later exploded still more vociferously at the Congresses of Czechoslovak Writers, in Prague, on May 22–24, and of Slovak Journalists, in Bratislava, on May 27–28. Although to some extent this unusual ferment was officially encouraged by the steps taken or about to be taken by the party, it soon got out of hand and became an independent force pushing events forward in the direction of further de-Stalinization.

The Slovak Writers' Congress at the end of April provided extraordinary evidence of what one writer (Karol Rosenbaum, newly elected Secretary of the Slovak Writers' Union) called "the revolutionary changes" which were taking place in society and in people's minds. The moment had come, he said, for a "clean slate," for which hopes had often been raised before, and just as often disappointed. He saw the meeting as a continuance of the spirit of the Writers' Congress of April, 1956, and as proof that there were forces sufficiently strong to prevent a return to the personality cult and its "inhuman" methods. The meeting offered writers an opportunity to release their pent-up emotions, to indicate their dissatisfaction with the progress of rehabilitation, and to assert their right to criticize errors in public life. It witnessed the moving speech by the writer, Laco Novomeský, who had been imprisoned for his alleged "bourgeois nationalism," and who was at long last restored to membership in the Union of Writers. He spoke openly of his friend, the executed Vlado

Clementis, and of the falsity of the charges levelled against him. Novomeský referred to the cult as something "monstrous and horrible," which had "wiped out trust, confidence, under-standing, yes, even loyalty, in the life and consciousness of thousands and thousands of people," and called for "the whole truth, and nothing but the truth." Others spoke of the immense damage done to Slovak literature by the unfounded charges of bourgeois nationalism against Slovak writers such as Novomeský and their removal from the literary scene, and called for a reassessment of the entire question of Slovak nationalism. A Czech spokesman, Jiří Hájek, spoke of the "stagnation" and "indifference" of Czech literature. Bitter at-tacks were made on those who had been responsible, in particular on Václav Kopecký, described by the author, Ladi-slav Mňačko, as "a symbol of those forces which, seven years ago, began to retard that advance and that spirit in our party and in our public life whose rebirth we are witnessing today."[8]

The Congress of the Union of Czechoslovak Writers at the end of May revealed that the mood of discontent was not con-fined to the Slovak writers alone, but included their Czech colleagues too. Even the party leadership was well aware of the temper of the writers and the unsatisfactory state of Czech and Slovak literature. Jiří Hendrych, a top party leader, in his address to the Congress, said that cult of per-sonality had "penetrated . . . the consciousness, thought and action of every one of us without distinction, even though in varying forms and intensity." A general improvement in the situation, and a raising of the quality of writing, required a painful process of "self-searching," and "the burning out to the roots of all remnants of the cult," said Ivan Skála, head of the Writers' Union. Another speaker, Vojtěch Mihálik, spoke of the indifference that had come to characterize not only literature but the whole of society, resulting from the conviction that "the divergence between the ideal and its realization is unsurmountable," from "the feeling of helpless-ness, from the feeling that any effort made to remedy the

---

[8]The proceedings were fully reported in the organ of the Slovak Writers, *Kulturný život*, April 27 and May 4, 1963.

existing weaknesses will have no direct influence upon the decisions made by 'those up there,'" and the "'philosophy' of don't-burn-your-fingers." Even *Rudé právo*, on the day of the opening of the Congress, lamented the "lack of civil and artistic courage, a definite distaste of 'burning one's fingers,' and . . . a tendency to give priority to the well-tried 'golden-mean,' the safe average."[9]

From the official point of view, the Congress was designed to mobilize the writers in support of the party's efforts, and draw them into a struggle for improving the state of literature and restoring faith in the party. Needless to say, control was to remain in the hands of the party, and the writers were considered merely its "closest aides" on the literary and ideological fronts. The writers were not to draw unwarranted conclusions from the struggle against the cult, nor accept bourgeois liberal ideas, but were to embody "party spirit" in their writing and in their publicly expressed attitudes on general problems. Although Skála in his closing speech concluded that the proceedings had indeed manifested this desired "party-mindedness," a reading of the text of the speeches as published in relatively full form in certain literary journals suggests that the writers went much further than anticipated and overstepped the bounds set by the party. Almost without exception, the participants were critical in the extreme, not only of the worst evils prevailing in the cult period, but also of their continuance right down to the present.[10]

Indeed the conference, like the second congress in 1956, could well be said to be acting as "the conscience of the nation." After 1956 this term had been officially denounced as arrogating to the writers the leading role which belonged only to the party. The term was now used again, although Mihálik,

---

[9]May 21, 1963.

[10]*Rudé právo* in effect admitted this fact by printing only the briefest excerpts of most of the speeches, and publicizing more fully only several ones, notably those by V. Mináč, Peter Karvaš, Vojtěch Mihálik, Josef Skvorecky, and Ladislav Stoll, and even in these cases omitting some of the most outspoken portions. A much fuller reporting was given in the two literary journals, *Kulturný život*, and *Literárni noviny*, from the end of April to early June.

in so doing, argued that the national conscience was being expressed, not "above" the party, but in identification with it. Speaker after speaker gave vent to the general public outrage at the horrors of the cult and the failure of the party to eliminate them since 1956, and spoke in individual ethical terms which had little to do with party-mindedness. Truth and freedom were words frequently invoked. Novomeský, for instance, spoke of the need for "a strict cult of uncompromising truth." Mináč referred to "the conditions of truth" which a writers' organization should create, and declared that "art is hampered by any terror, whether administrative, psychological or moral." The novelist Arnošt Lustig, referred to "the simple values of a human being, such as friendship, sincerity, courage, tenacity, endurance, and consideration for others."

Many of the speakers expressed their burning indignation over the so-called cult, that "terrible curse," in Novomeský's words, on the life of the country, and especially on literature, and a deep sense of shame for their own involvement in this system, and for their failure to resist it even after 1956. There was "an eternal stain on the good name of everyone of us," said Ladislav Mňačko, "for we all condemned Slánský, Clementis, Novomeský, and others." "Although I never believed that comrade Novomeský was an enemy of socialism," declared Zora Jesenká, "I did not do anything to have these accusations, which I considered false, examined. . . ." Even after Novomeský had been "secretly pardoned," said Karel Ptáčník, we were afraid to acknowledge him; only now are we "permitted to applaud. This permission to applaud was only given to us; we did not fight for it, and we did not even deserve it." "The tragedy of the whole situation lies not, or not only," declared Laco Novomeský himself, "in the fact that some believed more and some less a lie and accepted it, some in fear, some in the good faith that they were thus serving a correct cause. It lies in the fact, and this applies to us as writers and journalists in particular—that we tried to persuade our readers, of the correctness of the lie, that we misled and confused a whole generation, standing now outside this hall helpless, puzzled, uncertain and having no ground under its feet. To this generation we must return its confidence, trust, and truth; however, these we must find in ourselves first." Even a younger man, Anton Hykisch, too young to have been directly involved in the responsibility of the cult period, lamented that he had once "voted for the death of people about whom I, as a boy, knew no more than there was in the newspapers and about whom I know today—again only from the papers—that all was a lie, a calumny, a mistake, and a wrong."

In condemning the evils of the cult period, the writers went beyond the injustices done to individuals and scored the consequences on literature and life as a whole. Novomeský spoke bitterly of how the party had used its power "to sweep away from the history of Czech and Slovak culture an entire past," and in particular "the fruit of thirty years of Czech poetry" produced before the attainment of power. Michal Chorváth spoke of the terrible damage to Slovak literature by the attacks on bourgeois nationalism, and the *Dav* literary tradition, and by the elimination of such outstanding writers as Novomeský and others. Others spoke of "the rules and taboos" of the period, of the "fear" generated, "the black and white falsification of facts," the aversion and allergy towards the intelligentsia, the "bureaucratic narrow-mindedness," the "isolation" from the outside world, even from the socialist countries, and the "stagnation of our research." The main fault had been with "the system," said Jesenká, "which required unconditional confidence and unlimited trust, and which then abused this confidence and trust," and, said Vratislav Blažek, with the "method of direction which permitted an individual to appropriate the dictatorship of the proletariat." Mnačko, without naming him, pinned the responsibility directly on the political leader mainly responsible for the "ideological coercion" of the entire period, even after 1961, presumably Václav Kopecký. Others called him by name and also his chief lieutenant, Ladislav Stoll, eminent literary authority of the cult period, and powerful cultural manager. Stoll's present "silence" and his unwillingness to admit his errors, were openly deplored by several speakers, and his earlier book, *Thirty Years of Struggle of Czechoslovak Literature*, was sharply criticized.[11]

Most galling of all to most of the writers was the sense of frustration at the lateness and the slowness of the "rebirth" in Czechoslovak life after the death of Stalin. The danger of a relapse and of a recurrence of the old evils was also openly noted. Some doors had been opened in 1956, but were rapidly closed again after the Hungarian events and the campaign against revisionism. The "delayed end" of the Stalinist era had caused "enormous damage" especially in the moral and political sphere, "in the question of confidence," said Mináč. Mihálik spoke of "the lost opportunities" since Stalin's death, and even since 1956, and referred, in a passage published in *Rudé právo*, to "the forces which were braking progress and paralysing the most valuable moral capital of the revolution, the social conscience of the masses," and which "continued to exert their influence for a long time, and, to some extent still do so." Speakers cited specific cases of persecution of individual writers, the closing down of certain newspapers and journals, and the unjust condemnation of books, which had taken place since 1956 and even in more recent years. The failure of the Writers' Union to act as "a midwife assisting in the birth of progress" was lamented. "Instead of helping the new impulses to acquire full strength," the Union had "often nipped them in the bud, thus enabling the state of stagnation in the development of our art to continue," said Milan Kundera. The fact that the fight had really only begun was put strongly by Miroslav Válek as follows:

In this we cannot be satisfied with any *pars pro toto*. In the process of renewal and purification, which our party has begun to effect, we will evidently continue; it is necessary to continue this in a

[11]Stoll, while admitting that the spirit of the cult had strongly influenced his literary work during the period, defended its essential correctness, and refused to admit that "trust in the party" was equivalent to dogmatism. Some had died before the execution squad with the name of Stalin on their lips—were they dogmatists? he asked. The disclosures of the cult of personality had been a powerful shock but had not shaken our trust in the party, he declared.

downward and in an upward direction, in fact in every direction in which it is necessary.

As we have noted, there was more than one criticism of the continuing pernicious influence of persons who had been responsible for policy before 1956 and who remained in office even after the XXII Congress, not only persons such as Kopecký and Stoll at the top, but also leading cadres at other levels. A change in the leadership of the Writers' Union was demanded by several speakers. Many are afraid to stand up and say, "Comrades, I erred," declared Pavel Kohout. Many "who were the initiators or simply the convinced executors of administrative measures taken after 1956, and not rectified to this very day," remain in their positions. The strongest statement along these lines was made by Válek:

Many functionaries who were bearers of the cult hold their positions still, and have hardly changed in their thinking. Perhaps they stand up and cry, "Away with the Cult!" They raise a strict and critical finger and say: "Comrades, we have lived through a terrible time, in which you, too, have your share." And in doing this, they think: I shall get out of this somehow. In short, they act in accordance with the well-known Slovak proverb: *Nepovedz ty, povedia tebe.*[12]

A few days later, at the Congress of Slovak Journalists, held in Bratislava on May 27 and 28, a speech by Miro Hysko, a lecturer in the School of Journalism in Bratislava,[13] which was called by a commentator "a model of purely Communist criticism" created a sensation by denouncing those responsible for blocking "the process of revival" right down to the present, including the Prime Minister, Siroký. He lamented the fact that "the struggle for the restoration of Leninist norms after the XX Congress of the C.P.S.U. has been waged inconsistently here in Czechoslovakia, in a more or less declarative manner," and that "the fundamental questions which we should have solved as early as 1956 are facing us again today . . . with all the greater urgency." Noting that the era affected by anti-Leninist norms had lasted "roughly from 1949 to 1962," he

[12]Literally, "Speakest thou not, they will speak of thee"; or more freely, "Talk or be talked about."

[13]Substantially published in Slovak *Pravda*, June 3, 1963.

spoke of the well-known fact that "the promisingly developing process of revival, which began in our country after the
XX C.P.S.U. Congress, was being impeded by authoritative
intervention from the end of 1956 onwards." In Slovakia the
fight against bourgeois nationalism continued, and police and
illegal methods were still being used; some communists were
still held in prison, and the rehabilitation of others had been
kept secret. "And from 1956 to 1962 we constantly heard from
authoritative places of the systematic fight against the consequences of the cult of personality, and of the fact that, as far
as the re-examination of the trials was concerned, everything
was substantially in order." Again he turned to this theme, declaring that the issue was not merely the time of the trials, but
also the period after the XX C.P.S.U. Congress, and that what
was involved was not only the responsibility for the violation
of legality before 1956, but "the responsibility for the continuation of the methods of the cult of personality and in particular for putting up obstacles so that the conclusions of the XX
and XXII C.P.S.U. Congresses could not be fully applied in
our country." The attack on "bourgeois nationalism," which
was begun in 1950, had caused immense damage to Czech-
Slovak relations and was still continuing, must be ended, he
declared. "Without a correct settlement of the question of so-
called bourgeois nationalism, one cannot speak in Slovakia of
a consistent struggle against the cult of personality and against
its consequences. Without a critical examination of the conclusions of the ninth congress of the Slovak C.P., any measure of
rehabilitation is, and will remain, of necessity, a half-hearted
one."

Although admitting that the press and journalists were partly
responsible for the damage done before and after 1956, he
insisted on placing the major responsibility on the party leaders.[14] He cited the decisions of the 1950 congress of the

[14]"It must, therefore, be clear to every normally thinking person that
one measure of responsibility must be applied to those who inspired
these decisions, and who directed the whole propaganda campaign, and
another to those who carried them out and were subordinates in this
propaganda."

Communist party of Slovakia, especially Siroký's report on bourgeois nationalism on that occasion, and of the Central Committee meeting of February, 1951, based on the reports made by V. Kopecký and S. Bašťovánský concerning the anti-party conspiracy.[15] In particular, Kopecký "was not only one of the chief propagandists of the personality cult and executors of its methods prior to the XX Congress, but also continued on this road after the XX Congress of the C.P.S.U. right until his death, when as the man responsible for the whole ideological sector, he did everything possible to impede the liberating, anti-dogmatic process." (Even after his death in 1962, Hysko noted, a State Journalistic Prize bearing the name Kopecký was established.) In an obvious reference to Novotný's own effort in 1961 to escape blame, Hysko declared that he was ready to admit his own personal share of guilt "without commenting that I was not then in this or that leadership."

Hysko took up the delicate issue of the role of the journalists in public affairs and their relationship with the party. He strongly defended the right of writers to deal with all contemporary problems and to express "correct, i.e. Marxist-Leninist views even if they are in conflict with the subjectivist opinions of certain official persons." The journalists during the cult period, he said later, had "succumbed to the suggestive formula that the party, identified in our thoughts with the leading individuals, knew what it was doing" and that "we could not judge the matter so well and completely as the leading representatives of our party." Thus "we suppressed our own conscience" and accepted a "one-sided . . . interpretation of party discipline." In future, he concluded his speech, journalists should "respect only directives which are in no conflict

----

[15]Siroký's report was "not the result of an objective analysis of the facts" but "was based upon the *a priori* thesis of the inevitability of the bourgeois nationalist danger." "To this thesis all the facts had to be subordinated." This report is still the basis for a "non-objective appraisal of that whole phase of the party's and the nation's history from the twenties to 1950," "to the detriment of our historiography, history of literature and generally the whole field of education, both in and out of schools."

with the fundamental principles of socialist morality." This was in his opinion genuine "party-mindedness, understood not in a vulgar manner as servile subordination to the directing organ, but in the Leninist spirit, as conscious and devoted service to the aims of the Communist party, and as an objective judgment of all the facts from the standpoint of the unfalsified principles of Marxism-Leninism, which are equally binding on the directed and on those who direct."

This courageous statement was almost immediately followed by a major speech delivered by Novotný in Košice,[16] in Eastern Slovakia, remarkable for its defensive character, but at the same time for the savage offensive against the critics. He singled out Hysko by name, reprimanded other communists and non-party members for articles and for speeches at "various congresses," and criticized the editorial boards of *Kulturný život*, and even of the Slovak party organ, *Pravda*; he warned that the party would not sanction the publication of articles that were "an indirect attack on the policy of the party." Warning the critics of "the gulf" that was opening up between themselves and the party, Novotný ominously referred to "the dangerous path" on which some writers and editors had embarked. They had committed a serious breach of party principles by public discussion of "questions concerning which the Central Committee had stated completely clearly that they will be resolved within the party." "Let there be discussion and criticism," let opinions be explained, but "all this must be done within the framework (*v intencích*) of the party's policy, in the framework of the unity of people and country, in the framework of the struggle for the new and against the old, for the flourishing of creative constructive effort." As it was, he said, the critics were serving the interests of Western propaganda, in particular the efforts of Radio Free Europe to promote Czech-Slovak conflicts and a struggle for "freedom" in culture.

[16]*Rudé právo*, June 13. A reply to Hysko by two instructors in Marxism-Leninism was published in *Pravda* on June 12. They charged him with violating party discipline by discussing at a non-party gathering "purely internal party questions," and argued that much had been done, under party leadership, to overcome the effects of the cult.

Novotný was most angered by the allegations of the slowness of de-Stalinization. In an interview given on June 10th to the *London Times*, he roundly denied that there were any differences between himself and Khrushchev on this. In the Košice address Novotný denied that the party was only now "beginning to speak the truth" and tried to prove that great changes had been effected since 1956. Errors there had been, and injustices, but these had been corrected gradually and a final settlement was in the hands of the Supreme Court and the General Procurator.[17] These errors had not been corrected "under outside pressure" or "under the pressure of any small group of people." "The party itself had come forward with the demand for a struggle against the cult of personality. Only with the party, and under its leadership, and in its ranks, was it possible to conduct the struggle against the remains of the cult of personality so as to serve the interests of socialist society. Every attempt to conduct it outside the party or even against it led inevitably in its consequences to the very opposite." His speech disclosed, too, that although Slánský and some of his closest associates were to be given legal rehabilitation, they were not to be exonerated of their political responsibility, including the blame for setting in motion the "mill" of which they themselves had become the "sacrifice."

The fact that Novotný was speaking in Slovakia and that he addressed himself particularly to the Slovak question indicated that the relations of Czechs and Slovaks continued to be a serious problem which was closely linked to the question of

[17]The *Pravda* criticism of Hysko (June 12) had also defended the party's "gradual" approach to the question of the cult, arguing that, although it led to the temporary continuance of some cult methods, it had the positive result that these questions "were dealt with in organic connection with other questions fundamental and decisive from the point of view of constructing socialism" and that this had "enormous positive significance for the stability of the socialist camp in the period of the assault of international imperialism in the year 1956."

The authors of this article also argued that leading party cadres should not be judged solely or mainly on the bases of their view in the past, say, thirteen years ago, but mainly according to their present attitude and work, and especially their attitude to the party's twelfth congress decisions.

the revision of the trials of the 1950's. Novotný even went so far as to argue that the charges of bourgeois nationalism made by the ninth congress of the Slovak party had been basically correct, even if "insufficiently documented," and "not in all details justified." The Slovak leaders, such as Clementis, Novomeský and Husák, *had* committed errors of a nationalist character, and "breaches of party unity" at a time when they had occupied key positions in party and government. Moreover, there was still evidence of Slovak nationalism, said Novotný, citing recent criticisms by a writer, Kaliský, of alleged discrimination against Slovak firms. The party was, therefore, fully justified, he said, in pressing for a single economy, directed in a unified manner in the general interest of both Czechs and Slovaks. Indeed the gradual "approximation" of the two nations in the cultural as well as in the economic field, was the path that should be followed. There was no need for revision of the position of the Slovak organs under the constitution of 1960, since all that was required was fuller use by these organs of the competence granted to them in that document.

A leading article in *Rudé právo*, June 15, 1963, entitled "Leninist Principles Are the Supreme Law of Party Activity," dealt with the same topic. Admitting that the vestiges of the cult of personality had not been entirely eliminated, the article pleaded for an understanding of the complexity of the phenomenon, which was the result not merely of subjective factors in individuals, but of objective historic factors, such as the "cold war," and earlier, the "intoxication with victory" and the "feeling of omnipotence" resulting from the 1948 seizure of power. On these grounds, the editorial rejected "an individualistic and radical stance," which would call forth "distrust in the work of party organs and in their well-thought-out deliberate approach." Later, the article denounced "superficial and cheap demagogy, based purely on emotional grounds, which reduces complicated problems of the cult to, and makes them synonymous (*jednoznačně*) with, this responsibility" (of individuals), and denounced "an emotional approach, in the evaluation of any historical phenomenon," which prevented an "objective analysis" in "the evaluation of individual persons, as well as of whole epochs." It was not surprising "that some quarters would greet with pleasure a 'rehabilitation' that would completely condemn everything which happened here in the past, and which would be designed to demonstrate the correctness of the attacks of our enemies on party policy," as had happened after the XX Congress of the C.P.S.U. "Our enemies are anticipating that people will condemn, together with the cult, the party, socialism, the general line of construction of socialism and its further development in our country. They are counting precisely on a one-sided emotional approach of people to past errors."

The article sought in particular to rebut the charges that the party had done nothing, or was only just beginning, to eliminate the personality cult. The revision of the main political trials had not taken place sooner for reasons that had been given at the twelfth congress, it was argued. Those who were "dissatisfied with the alleged 'Stalinism' of our party" were reminded how much had already been done and that the party itself had been "the initiator of the struggle" and was directing it. The party could not, therefore, allow this struggle to be "belittled by the fact that its bearers should become some isolated *literati* who transferred it to the level of unrequired speculation and abstract scholastic disputes, designed to demonstrate their own mentorial relationship to the party and society, and their characteristic opportunism based on bombastic verbal effects." What was required of all members was "a party approach," i.e. "defending and carrying out in a responsible and disciplined fashion the line worked out by the party congress and concretized by decisions of the Central Committee." The party was "not a discussion club" and required strict discipline. The party "will not revise its political line, which life had fully confirmed," although this did not mean that it might not "correct certain conclusions drawn from actions of party organs in the past." The views of certain speakers at the Congress of Journalists identifying the struggle against the cult and rehabilitation with the denial of bourgeois nationalism ignored the actual dangers of nationalism in

Slovakia and cast in doubt the official policy on the national question.

It is difficult, from a distance, to estimate the full significance of the events described, or to predict the ultimate consequences. In ensuing months, speeches by top party leaders testified to their continuing concern over the critical tone of some writers and newspapers, and persistent fear of its political implications. Hendrych, for instance, at the end of June, again struck out sharply at the false ideas that the time between 1956 and 1962 had been wasted, and that the writers formed "the leading ideological centre of our society," and claimed that the party alone was "the conscience of the nation."[18] The Slovak leader, Dubček, attacked Hysko again personally for publicly discussing internal party questions at the Congress of Journalists, and extended his onslaught to "undisciplined and impatient comrades who . . . not waiting for the decision of the Supreme Court, try to create the impression that they, and not the Central Committee, were consistently struggling for the rehabilitation of unjustly condemned persons and for the correction of errors."[19]

In spite of such strong and public condemnation, the writers gave little evidence of willingness to retreat from their advanced positions. The Union of Writers, under its new leaders, and literary newspapers, especially *Kulturný život*, did not relax their critical approach to questions of public life. The Writers' Congress continued to be praised for its contributions. No changes were made in the editorial boards of the dissident journals, and outspoken articles and vigorous debates continued to be published. In all fields, such as, for instance, in economics, law, and history, in art, philosophy, and literature, there was a thorough-going critique of the methods and the conclusions of the Stalinist period, and a steady effort to reappraise previously accepted knowledge in those fields. The views of Stoll, for instance, continued to be sharply criticized. A constant stream of articles sought to re-evaluate such crucial

[18]*Rudé Právo*, June 29, 1963. Cf. articles by Jan Fojtík, *ibid.*, July 11, 1963, and Sept. 7, 1963.
[19]*Ibid.*, June 27, 1963.

episodes of the party's past as the Slovak uprising in 1943, the wartime resistance and the Prague uprising of 1945, and the policies of the party after 1948. To some extent, this self-examination was officially sponsored, as part of the proclaimed goal of eliminating all vestiges of the period of the cult. This freer and more rational approach to intellectual problems may, however, ultimately go far beyond the limits originally set by the authorities. In this sense the long-term intellectual impact of the XXII Congress is likely to be continuing and immense, and is at the present time unpredictable.

Meanwhile, the final results of the re-examination of the political trials were, at long last, published in a brief, dry report, which appeared in *Rudé právo*, on August 22, 1963. Coming as it did after such long delay and after so much public clamour, it was not likely to strengthen the position of the Novotný leadership, which seemed to have been brought around to this action slowly and reluctantly. Moreover, of the thousands of persons who had suffered in the period of the trials, only 481 cases had been re-examined since 1955, and only about 70 were referred to by name, all of them party members at the time of their arrest. The report was nonetheless explosive in its implications, for it cancelled the indictment against all the victims of the main trials of the fifties, and thus admitted that these had been nothing but a travesty of justice. Absolved of all the charges that had led to their execution were Rudolf Slánský and his ten fellow victims, including Vlado Clementis, and other leaders. Also vindicated were other persons who had been tried in groups, including Maria Svermová, and top party *apparatchiki*; Husák, Novomeský, and other Slovak leaders; Josef Goldman, and associates in central planning and industrial management; certain lesser party officers, including Richard Slánský; and some army generals. In certain cases, the possibility of actual abuse of power or breach of legality was mentioned, but death, or the 1960 amnesty, made unnecessary further legal proceedings. In the case of one former high party official, Jarmila Tausiggová, it was said, the investigation had not yet been completed. As for Slánský himself, he was declared responsible for permit-

ting and concealing "breaches of legality," and along with a
number of others, his expulsion from the party was not res-
cinded, even posthumously.[20] Although no mention was made
of this in the report, some of the Slovak leaders, while re-
admitted to the party, were not restored to membership in the
Central Committee because of political failings in the earlier
period, and their alleged "bourgeois nationalism" was subject
to continued criticism.[21]

A month later, a reshuffle of government and party commands occurred, suggesting a further crumbling of the position of the older leadership contaminated by the cult and its
results. Most notable of all was the removal from the premiership of Siroký, who had borne heavy responsibility throughout
the Gottwald period, and after, and had been publicly criticized during the Congress of Journalists. He was dropped for
"inadequacies in his work," "insufficient implementation of the
party line in directing the activity of the government," and
"certain errors in his political activity in the past." He was
also excluded from the party Presidium. Another old-timer,
the Slovak Duriš, was replaced as Minister of Finance, and
excluded from the Central Committee. Dolanský, an associate
of Gottwald's from 1929 and post-war top leader, was relieved
of his position as Deputy Chairman of the government, and
from his office as chairman of a state committee on science
but was appointed chairman of the new party commission on
the standard of living. Ludmila Jankovcová, one-time Social
Democrat, and member of the C.P.C. leadership after the
fusion, ceased to be Deputy Chairman of the government and
candidate in the party Presidium. In varying degrees, these
shifts represented a sloughing off of older leaders who had

[20]In a long article in *Rudé právo*, Aug. 7, 1963, it was revealed that
two prominent officials from the trial period, Cepicka, Minister of
National Defence, and L. Kopřiva, Minister of Public Security, had
been expelled from the party. No other action was apparently taken
against them. It should also be noted that Bacílek and Köhler remained
party members, and were even elected to parliamentary committees.

[21]See speeches by Dubček and Hendrych, *Rudé právo*, June 27 and
29, 1963.

shouldered heavy responsibility before and after 1956. More difficult to evaluate was the departure of Císař from the secretariat of the C.P.C., and his appointment as Minister of Education and Culture, which seemed to represent a substantial demotion. His role in de-Stalinization in 1963 had been considerable, but whether as a spokesman of the Novotný line, or an advocate of a more accelerated course, was not easy to determine. Into the place of Siroký as Prime Minister stepped a Slovak party veteran, Jozef Lenárt, a leader of post-1958 vintage, who had until then been head of the Slovak Board of Commissioners, and a member of the Slovak party Presidium, its secretariat, and the C.P.C. Presidium.

The XXII Congress had a delayed reaction in Czechoslovakia. After a long period of passivity, the "time bomb" of the renewed assault on Stalinism began to explode early in 1963. Verbal and symbolic de-Stalinization, coupled with the mounting tide of public discontent, produced an ever greater confidence of public utterance and an ever broader and deeper stream of criticism. Party members, notably the writers and journalists, courageously asserted their own viewpoint in opposition to that of the leadership, and began to give sharper and sharper expression to their feelings of guilt and remorse, and their outrage at the slowness of change. Throughout 1963 Novotný was subjected to vocal criticism for his failure to break the hold of Stalinism on national life, to rehabilitate publicly those who had suffered most in the era of repression, and to punish those who had borne the main burden of responsibility in that era. Most vehemently did the Slovak writers call for greater freedom in their national life, and for the erasing of the charges of "bourgeois nationalism" on which the purge of leading Slovak personalities had been based. Step by step, Novotný had had to retreat before these waves of protest, finally finding himself forced to rehabilitate almost all the victims of the trials of the fifties, and even to remove from the leadership some of his key associates. In eliminating those most tarred with the brush of Stalinism, especially

Bacílek and Siroký, Novotný was yielding to, and at the same time seeking to disarm, the critics of his course of slow de-Stalinization. At the same time, successive retreats before the tide of public opinion, in particular the removal of Siroký, might in the end undermine his own position and destroy his hold on power. It is almost certain that the final effects of the XXII Congress have not made themselves felt in Czechoslovakia.[22]

[22]See pp. 156–7 below. See also my chapter, "Czechoslovakia's Place in the Communist Bloc," in Adam Bromke, *The Communist States at the Crossroads* (New York, 1964).

8

THE CHANGING SOVIET BLOC *

THE IMAGES OF INTERNATIONAL COMMUNISM which are still cast
on the screen of our minds are no longer accurate reflections of
the reality of this phenomenon. We visualize world communism as a unified and monolithic "bloc" or "camp," directed
from a single centre, Moscow, and by a single man, Lenin,
Stalin, or Khrushchev. Or we think of it in astronomical terms
as a group of man-made satellites which travel in pre-ordained
orbits from the Moscow launching pad. We also sometimes
think of world communism as an empire, whose dependent
territories, in Asia and Europe, are strictly controlled by the
metropolitan country, the U.S.S.R. or sometimes as a universal
Church hierarchical in structure, with a Muscovite pontiff
guarding the sacred writ against heresy and excommunicating
the heretic when necessary.

In the past none of these images was entirely removed from
the reality; yet all of them have lost much of their capacity
to reflect the changed character of world communism. Even
the term "bloc" has lost most of its validity. World communism
is certainly no longer a *Soviet* bloc, dominated by Moscow,
but at the best a Sino-Soviet bloc, with two centres of authority, Moscow and Peking. At the worst, it seems likely at any
time to dissolve into two separate and competing blocs. Nor
is communism any longer uniform and monolithic in its character; it presents an increasingly variegated pattern, each of
its members following its own distinctive course.

Putting aside for the moment the problem of definition,

*Published in Richard Pipes *et al., The Changing Communist World*
(United Nations Association in Canada, Toronto, 1963).

what I propose to discuss is world communism, an international system made up of the communist states and the Communist parties of the entire world. At present this comprises fourteen states, including, in Europe, the U.S.S.R. and its eight communist neighbours, from East Germany down to Yugoslavia and Albania; in Asia, China, and three other (North Korea, North Vietnam, and Mongolia); and in the Americas, Cuba, which has chosen to place itself in the ranks of world communism through the decision of its leader, Castro. These are the states termed by Moscow, in its 1963 May Day slogans, the countries which are "building socialism," and which are described in Soviet scholarship and propaganda as "the world socialist system."

Closely associated is what calls itself "the international communist and working class movement," made up of 87 parties and 36,000,000 members, in all continents and almost all countries of the world. Among its most massive and influential contingents are the Italian and French Communist parties in Europe, and the Indonesian Communist party in Asia. If we are to use the term "Soviet bloc" at all, we cannot apply it to this powerful grouping of states and parties, but at most to the inner group of seven states in Europe (excluding at present Albania and Yugoslavia), which are part of the tightly knit Warsaw military alliance, headed by the Soviet Union, and of the Council for Economic Mutual Assistance, or Comecon.

This vast and heterogeneous assemblage of states and parties may best be called, not a bloc or empire, not an alliance or church, but, using a much more neutral and general term, the international communist system.[1] It is a global grouping, the constituent parts of which are bound together by certain common interests and certain common doctrines, as well as, in the case of the states, by general similarity of their political and economic institutions. Yet they exhibit considerable differences of interest, of policies, and of institutions, and possess varying degrees of independence of action in their domestic and even their foreign policies.

[1]G. Modelski uses this term, but with a somewhat different meaning in *The Communist International System* (Princeton, 1960).

The system lacks the strict subordination to a single centre characteristic of an empire, or in the realm of doctrine, of a Church. It lacks the tight organizational structure and unity of outlook of a bloc, or even of an alliance, although the inner group of seven, headed by the Soviet Union, comes closest to that familiar type of international organization. It may be compared roughly with other international systems, such as the United Nations, or the Atlantic community of nations, or the Inter-American system, or the Arab League, but exhibits its own distinctive characteristics. In some ways, it resembles the British Commonwealth of Nations, a similarity recognized perhaps by the communists themselves in their use of the term "the commonwealth (*sodruzhestvo*) of socialist nations" to describe their system as it has evolved since the death of Stalin. Here, too, however, the analogy is imperfect indeed, and the communist system has to be thought of as *sui generis*.

At the outset, then, I have discarded two thirds of my title. World communism is neither Soviet nor a bloc. But it *is* changing, and so rapidly that we often fail to readjust our perception of it, and still think of it in terms of old *clichés* no longer appropriate. As long as there was only one communist state, the U.S.S.R., to which the Communist parties of the world, organized in the Communist International, were strictly subordinated, there was truth in the image of world communism as a single, undivided bloc or empire. This conception of unity, devised by Lenin and forged by Stalin into an organizational reality, did characterize world communism down to the outbreak of World War II. Only the Chinese Communist party under Mao Tse-tung stood somewhat apart, as an independent although closely allied entity.

Even before the war, there was some recognition by Stalin himself, of the need to recognize the increasing diversity of world communism and to adjust the organization of the Comintern to this. On the whole, however, the Comintern, down to its demise in 1943, was an instrument used to enforce on all communists and all Communist parties the strictest of discipline to the single centre in Moscow. The leadership of these parties, except for that of the Chinese, was changed at will by

Moscow, and in case of extreme need, an entire party, such as the Polish, was dissolved and its leaders executed.

It was the emergence of the new communist states in Europe after 1944, and in Asia, after 1949, that proved to be the solvent which in the end produced the metamorphosis of the original Moscow-centred communist movement. At first the decomposing effect of the existence of not one but ten, and by 1952, thirteen communist states, was veiled from view by two facts. In the first place, the European satellites, although following a self-proclaimed "national path" to socialism, were for the most part doing so at the behest of, and with the sanction of, Moscow, most of them having been brought into existence by the action of the Soviet Union in the war and post-war period. In the second place, even in those cases where communism had been established largely by indigenous forces and autonomous action, notably in China, Vietnam, and Yugoslavia, and in a modified degree, Albania, loyalty to Moscow was proclaimed by the leadership, and for the most part reflected in the course of policy followed. Moreover, Stalin had at his disposal an array of varied controls (political, economic, military, police, ideological, and so on), which were effective in keeping most of these states in line.

The monolithic character of world communism reached a high point in the closing years of Stalin's life, with the formation of the Cominform, embracing the European satellites and the French and Italian parties, and with the abandonment by the former of their national path to socialism and their adoption of a new slogan, "the Soviet model." Even at this time, however, the germs of a new infection, "national communism," were evident in what Professor Brzezinski has called "domesticism," the orientation of otherwise loyal and devoted parties to domestic needs and interests, without sacrifice of the broader needs and interests of communism as defined by Moscow.[2]

A much more serious manifestation of the same disease was, however, the defection of Yugoslavia from the bloc in 1948,

[2] Z. Brzezinski, *The Soviet Bloc, Unity and Conflict* (Harvard, 1960), p. 52.

and its setting out on a course of independent action. Long before the death of Stalin and the rise of the Sino-Soviet divergence, it was this action of a satellite state which set the ball moving in the direction of the present system of world communism. The world witnessed at that time not only the emergence of an independent communist state, free of Soviet control, but also the gradual evolution of a communist society differing in important aspects of its organization and policy from the Soviet model.

The rest of the Soviet bloc began to take on an even more monolithic form with the formation of the Warsaw military alliance and the Comecon, and the adoption of the policy of strict conformity within the camp. But Yugoslavia now offered a permanent challenge, in the form of "national communism," to this conformism and subordination, and a standing alternative model of future relations within the communist world system. Yugoslavia was, however, too small and weak to bring about at this time significant changes in the camp itself. Only a year later, the rise of communism to power in China, possessing all the latent strength of a great power, contained even greater potential for a disintegration of the original Soviet camp.

The full implications of this potentiality of national communism were realized only in the wake of the decomposition of the Stalinist system which resulted from the death of Stalin and the deliberate effort by his successor, Khrushchev, to remodel the relations of world communism on what he thought would be a sounder and more viable pattern. The dissolution of the Cominform, the *rapprochement* with Tito and Yugoslavia in 1955, the recognition of the heretical doctrine of "many paths to socialism," were followed by the assault on Stalin and Stalinism, in February, 1956, and the loosening of many of the police and other controls in the European satellites. All these measures were designed to further the formation of what was called, as early as 1955, the "commonwealth of socialist nations."[3]

[3]*Kommunist,* No. 14, cited by Brzezinski, *The Soviet Bloc,* p. 179.

Although Khrushchev had certainly not become First Secretary to preside over the liquidation of the communist empire inherited from his predecessor, he did intend to try to transform it into a grouping in which the members, in exchange for some limited degree of autonomy, would recognize a continuing "inequality of function" in the form of Soviet primacy and Soviet leadership. This was not identical with the pattern of bloc relations desired by Tito, who wished complete independence within a voluntary alliance of equals, but it was close enough to tempt him into the belief that Khrushchev's conception would eventually be brought into line with his own. For a short period, prior to the Hungarian and Polish events of 1955–56, the role of Tito greatly expanded, as he sought to push Khrushchev further along the road of de-Stalinization, especially in the European satellites such as Hungary, and to persuade him to accept the Soviet-Yugoslav relationship of parity as the model for the entire bloc.

Both Tito's conception of a commonwealth of free and independent communist nations and Khrushchev's notion of a commonwealth of subordinate dominions perished in the catastrophe of Hungary. A modified form of autonomy within unity was established, however, in the compromise reached between Poland and the Soviet Union in 1956, offering a new version of national communism. A new stage had been reached in world communism, with one state, Yugoslavia, still independent and at variance with important policies of the U.S.S.R. and another, Poland, enjoying some autonomy, especially in its domestic policies, and capable of taking its own stance in inner-bloc discussions of common policies.

The role of China was, therefore, not chronologically the initial factor in leading to the transformation of world communism. It was the countries of Eastern Europe that produced the first shifts in the monolithic character of world communism and paved the way for what has happened since.

China had, however, already emerged as a country exerting substantial influence on bloc policy and even on Eastern European affairs as a result of the crisis of 1956. At first China gave support to Polish and Hungarian efforts to secure an

improved position. After the Hungarian experience she moved
to the other extreme and became an exponent of the unity and
uniformity of the bloc, and of Soviet leadership. At the communist conference of 1957, indeed, China emerged as a mediating force in the solidification of the bloc under Soviet direction.
Chinese influence moved in the direction of a centralist
organization of the bloc, more centralist than that espoused
by Khrushchev in the pre-1956 days, and of a total rejection
of the Titoist conception of a loose commonwealth of equal
and independent members. Within a year, however, the emergence of the Sino-Soviet conflict posed anew the question of
leadership and control of the bloc, and indeed the very nature
of the system of world communism.

Since 1958, the situation in the camp of world communism
has been described as one of "divergent unity." Unity is still
maintained, at least in the form of a broad consensus on policy
and doctrine as adumbrated in the communist declarations of
1957 and 1960, and in a constant reiteration of the need for
solidarity on the part of all members.[4] But serious cracks
had already become visible on the surface of unity. Most
notable of course, was the profound divergence of viewpoint
between China and the Soviet Union, expressing itself at first
esoterically in the language of doctrinal debate, and later in
open polemics. In the absence of a Stalin able to lay down a
binding interpretation of doctrine and the essentials of common policy, Mao and Khrushchev have been engaged in a war
of words increasing in its intensity and in its openness. Nor
does Khrushchev have at his disposal the instruments of control, organizational and political, that his predecessor had at
hand to enforce obedience to his will.

The conflict was not confined to the two giants of the communist camp. Other lesser powers played their role. Yugoslavia, still in sharp conflict with the Soviet Union as late as 1961,
and the target of virulent attack by China, steadily moved
closer to the former and away from China. At the same time
its closest neighbour, little Albania, has emerged as the only

[4]Yugoslavia did not sign either document, although she accepts some
of the principles set forth.

partner of China in Europe. In Asia in turn, Mongolia is the only partner of the Soviet Union against China; whereas North Korea, and to an increasing degree North Vietnam, have become supporters of China.

Some parties teetered on the fence, and eventually toppled down on one side or other, as the Cubans and Vietnamese after some hesitation seem to have fallen on the Soviet and the Chinese side respectively. The non-governing parties of world communism have also moved in one or other direction, some of them, such as the Indian, the French, and the Italian, supporting the position of the Soviet Union, and others, such as the Indonesian and Japanese, supporting China. There has been, therefore, a distinct but not exclusive tendency towards a geographical alignment, with Asian parties tending to support China, and European parties, as well as African, Arab, and Latin American, tending to support Soviet Russia.

There has been also a propensity of parties to split internally, with pro-Chinese and pro-Russian wings emerging. Although there is no clear evidence of such an intra-party division in either China or the Soviet Union, there are probably some Chinese communists who sympathize with Moscow, and at least some Russian or East European communists who entertain sympathies for the Chinese position. The situation described by the Italian communist, Togliatti, in 1956, as "polycentrism," has thus become "an established fact," with at least two major centres of authority and a number of minor centres already in existence, and the future emergence of other centres a more or less certain probability.[5]

Organizationally, the international communist system manifests a structure basically different to that which existed under Stalin. Indeed on the surface it appears to have become a rather loose and inchoate system, lacking a tight-knit organization such as the Comintern or the Cominform. It must, however, be noted that important as the Comintern was as an administrative mechanism for maintaining unity and uniformity within the pre-war communist movement, the real guar-

[5]Walter Z. Laqueur, "The Schism," in an issue of *Survey* devoted to polycentrism, No. 42 (June, 1962), p. 8.

antee of this unity was the dominant position of the Soviet Union and the loyalty and obedience of the national party leaders to Moscow. The unity was therefore not destroyed by the dissolution of the Comintern in 1943, nor was it seriously strengthened by the creation of the Cominform in 1947.

Indeed, after the war, control by Moscow of the states of Eastern Europe was largely based on its real sources of power, such as military occupation or encirclement, police permeation, economic absorption, as well as the continuing loyalty of the national leaders and the ideological cement set by Stalin's monopoly of the interpretation of doctrine. The absence of the Comintern did not lead to serious defections from the world movement, nor did the existence of the Cominform prevent the defection of what had been the most loyal of satellites, Yugoslavia. As suggested earlier, the ultimate solvent of the unity of world communism has been the fact of the existence of separate communist régimes, each enjoying power in its own state, and inevitably developing its own policies in the light of differing national circumstances. Whether a tighter organization would have warded off serious disunity seems doubtful, although it might have contributed something to the compromising of differences.

At the present time the organizational structure of world communism is multi-form—shadowy and ill-defined in some respects, systematic and precise in others. As far as the inner core of the Soviet bloc is concerned, unity is based on the Warsaw military alliance and its high command and the intricate system of Comecon and its subordinate commissions for economic co-ordination and division of labour. The solid foundation of these institutions is the might of the Soviet army, its occupation of the territory of certain of the bloc members (East Germany, Poland, and Hungary), and the great economic influence exerted by the Soviet Union through foreign trade and aid.

Nonetheless, even within this inner group, each member still possesses its own armed forces and its own national economy, so that a full merging of the seven states has not been effected. The defection of members from the Warsaw

Pact and from Comecon is not impossible, as the case of Albania demonstrates. Bilateral associations knit together the seven states of the inner core somewhat further, producing a constant interchange of top leaders and party *apparatchiki*, as well as government officials and technical specialists. A visit by Khrushchev to Sofia or Prague, or by all the East European First Secretaries to Moscow or to each other's party congresses, provides as effective an organizational link as the pre-war Comintern, and one more in tune with the increasingly autonomous position of these states. Nor is it without significance that the decisions of the C.P.S.U., especially those of its Congress and Central Committee, and the speeches of Khrushchev, are openly accepted as guiding instructions for the parties outside the Soviet Union.

It can be argued therefore that the unorganized appearance of the world communist system is deceptive and veils a highly systematized and ordered unity of action. Nonetheless, to an increasing extent the authority exercised by the Soviet Union in the world communist system, even within its inner core, is taking the form, not of direct control, as in the old days, but of indirect influence, and can therefore be thrown off in part or in whole by any of its members, as in the case of Albania. This is even more true of the more remote members of the system, such as the Asian states, notably powerful China, or the non-governing parties, such as the Italian or Indonesian, with their own views of the best course to follow. Very few of the states concerned are members of administrative mechanisms such as the Warsaw Pact or Comecon;[6] only some of them have treaties of alliance with the U.S.S.R. The only organizational link between them, apart from bilateral talks, is the occasional gathering in Moscow of the Communist parties of the world, such as that held in 1957, and in 1960, and the one being discussed in connection with the Sino-Soviet dispute.[7] The Soviet Union is not without great influence, especially of an ideologi-

---

[6]Mongolia was admitted to Comecon as a full member.

[7]The journal *Problemy mira i sotsializma* (Problems of Peace and Socialism), published in Prague, is another important link. It has ceased to appear in Albanian and Chinese.

cal and economic character, on all the members, but it is an influence that is not decisive or inescapable.

The position of Cuba illustrates the peculiar nature of world communism. This country is not linked organizationally in either the Warsaw alliance or the Comecon, nor has it been a member of previous world conferences. One can define its relationship mainly in terms of Soviet economic and military assistance, the promise of aid in case of attack, and the proclamation of loyalty by Castro to Marxism-Leninism. The month-long visit by Castro to the U.S.S.R. in 1963 seems to have tied him firmly to Moscow, but not in a manner that prevents a relatively easy withdrawal if the spirit should move him. At the other extreme, the case of East Germany illustrates a different type of relationship, a close and intimate one based on the indispensability for Ulbricht, and for the very existence of his régime, of the continued presence of Soviet troops on East German territory. This requires him to tone down and moderate his own distinctive views of the solution of the Berlin question.

Yugoslavia is still another paradoxical case—an independent country, a member of neither the Warsaw Pact nor Comecon, not subject to decisive Soviet military and economic influence, and insistent on its own distinctive ideological and political position. Nonetheless Yugoslavia has recently drawn somewhat nearer to the inner core. It seems very doubtful that Tito will join the inner bloc as a full member; but even if he did, it would be a voluntary adhesion, preserving complete independence, and would have a great potential impact on the other members of the bloc.

It is within this greatly changed world communist system that the dispute between the Chinese and the Russians has been taking place these past years. It has been in a large measure a struggle for power, a contest for leadership. Who will "lead" the bloc? Khrushchev has gone so far as to say (January 6, 1961), that it is now "impossible to lead all the socialist countries and Communist parties from any single centre."[8] This disclaimer in effect sought to avoid accepting

[8]*Pravda*, Jan. 25, 1961.

the challenge of the Chinese to modify his own policy in domestic, bloc, and foreign affairs—in other words, to free himself from the obligations of being a leader responsible to an organized and unified movement.

In fact, however, the Soviet party has never ceased to assert the traditional authority of the Communist party of the Soviet Union and the U.S.S.R. to act as the guiding and directing force of the whole communist world movement. Paradoxically, there is no member of the system, except Yugoslavia, that challenges in words the special position enjoyed by the U.S.S.R. and its vanguard, the C.P.S.U.; even China and Albania accept this principle of Soviet primacy.[9] Indeed, the Chinese and the Albanians are seeking not so much to displace the Soviet Union from its leading role, as to press it to lead in a different direction. This is a struggle over policy; yet the Chinese challenge to Soviet policy, and to majority communist policy, cannot but be in effect a challenge to Soviet leadership suggesting that the Chinese themselves know best where to lead and, therefore, how to lead.

Not only is the question of leadership involved, but also the matter of discipline and autonomy, i.e., the degree to which each party may follow its own path at home and abroad, and determine, independently of Moscow, its own course of action. Although all proclaim not only the necessity of unity, but also the importance of independence and equality for the members, it is clear that just as the Chinese do not relish acceptance of the Soviet leadership as at present formulated, neither do the Soviets wish to permit or recognize the right of the Chinese to an independent position. The C.P.S.U. has rejected the Chinese doctrine of the right of the minority to seek to change the "general line" of the movement as a whole, and has insisted on the necessity of disciplined obedience to that line as set forth by the world communist system, in effect that is, by the C.P.S.U. and the U.S.S.R.[10]

[9]Cf. Puniša Perović, "On Problems of Leadership and International Relations in the International Workers' Movement," *Naša Stvarnost* (March, 1962).

[10]*Pravda*, Jan. 7, 1963.

The struggle for power and leadership within the system merges with the contest for power and leadership within each country. Each party command seeks, within the other parties, to promote the fortunes of these persons favourable to its own position, usually without much success. Nonetheless the continued existence of the Albanian leadership, just as that of the Yugoslav in 1948, is at stake in the conflict with the Soviet Union. Directly involved is the question—who will control the Albanian party—Moscow or Tirana? and if Tirana, which leader? Although this is less acutely the case in the dispute between China and the Soviet Union, the positions of Mao Tse-tung and of Khrushchev are to some extent linked with the outcome of the struggle between the parties.

The great doctrinal debate between the Soviet Union and China has not, however, been a mere camouflage for a battle for power and position by the rival parties and leaders. Nor has it centred exclusively on the question of the leadership and organization of world communism. It has involved profound divergences of view between the two countries and their supporters on fundamental issues of policy, both at home and abroad. Although both consider themselves loyal disciples of a common doctrinal faith, Marxism-Leninism, they differ profoundly on the interpretation of this faith, and its application to their own conditions and to the contemporary world.

This is not the first occasion in history in which those who profess the same faith have found that this has brought conflict rather than co-operation. Deep diversity in the circumstances of each country, basic contrasts in revolutionary background, differing levels of economic development and political modernization, as well as the personality traits of rival leaders, have made inevitable the emergence of divergences among communists. Khrushchev himself has recognized "that among communists of different countries, there can appear a different understanding of even quite serious questions. . . . Although this is not an entirely pleasant phenomenon, we must reckon with it as with a real fact."[11] Moreover, as the history of communism has itself demonstrated (although Khrushchev has

[11]*Ibid.*, Jan. 17, 1963.

not admitted this), there was bound to emerge within each party and its leading corps different conceptions of strategy and tactics and hence competing factions, each seeking to imbue the party with its own views.

The controversy, carried on for some time in an obscure, semantic way, with the real targets veiled in doctrinal camouflage, has burst into open polemics. Even before this, the Western student, as well as the communist, sophisticated in Aesopian language, could piece together the main points of conflict and deduce the target of the mutual attacks. The recent book by Donald Zagoria, *The Sino-Soviet Conflict, 1956–1961* (Princeton, 1962), analysed the technique of "esoteric communication" employed by communist leaders and newspapers, and sets forth in the fullest detail the substance of the conflict.

Strangely enough, the real dispute was at first obscured to a considerable extent for the citizens of the communist world. For a long time even the party member could only vaguely sense the existence of a conflict in which his own party leadership was directly involved. Even now, with all open polemics being conducted, the communist citizen cannot grasp the full meaning of the controversy, as the major documents from both sides have not been published in the press.

On the whole the Western citizen has long been forewarned of the developing conflict and has a fairly clear idea of the issues involved. There has been, however, the additional stumbling block that the entire debate has been conducted in ideological terms, with each side claiming to be the orthodox interpreter of the doctrine of Marxism-Leninism. It is difficult for a Western observer to realize that communists take these matters seriously and look at the world through the prism of their faith. There is little doubt that the doctrinal controversy reflects the deep commitments of the communists to their beliefs and their conviction that a wrong interpretation of the doctrine must be combatted with the right one. We should recall that in the past great Churches, both in West and East, have been split asunder on fine points of doctrine that seem on the surface trivial and meaningless.

Unlike the mediaeval scholastics, who argued about how many angels could dance on the head of a pin, the communist debaters are practical political actors worrying over concrete political problems. To a great extent their dialogue, although expressed in ideological terms, has involved real questions of strategy and tactics, of immense magnitude.

It is impossible to do more than to list some of the basic points of controversy that divide the communist world, and in particular the Chinese and the Russians. Some are matters of domestic policy, such as the Chinese agricultural communes, rejected by the Soviet Union as ineffective and heretical. Khrushchev's own domestic course has been subjected to Chinese criticism as too "economic" in character, that is, too pragmatic and empirical, and departing from the necessary political orthodoxy demanded by Leninism. Although some national peculiarities are to be tolerated, in both the Chinese and Soviet views, each charges the other with passing beyond the limit of tolerable deviation.

Even more critical are problems of foreign policy: the possibility of coexistence, of disarmament and nuclear controls, the desirability of summit meetings and great power negotiations, and of aid to the developing countries, and specific issues such as Cuba and the Sino-Indian frontier conflict. Time and again, on these matters, the Chinese and the Russians have found themselves on opposite sides of the debate. And there have also been profound differences of view over *the strategy of future revolution*, a traditional bone of contention among communists, with conflicting beliefs as to the swiftness of the transition to revolution, the amount of support to be given to revolutionary movements, the question of leadership by the working class and relations with other classes such as the so-called "national bourgeoisie." China has in particular tended to advance her own experience as a model particularly suitable for application to Asia and other backward continents.

Special attention should be given to an important but confusing bone of contention, namely Stalinism and de-Stalinization. The issue was first raised by Khrushchev's assault on Stalinism and the "cult of personality" at the XX Party Congress in 1956, and his renewed onslaught at the XXII Congress in 1961, extended to include the alleged continuance of Stalinism in Albania. By implication, China and the entire "dogmatic" or "sectarian" deviation was linked with Stalinism. There is little doubt that the Khrushchev strategy of de-Stalinization was thoroughly disliked by the Chinese from the beginning, producing as it did unpredictable shocks to the unity of the world communist movement and the stability of certain communist régimes. China, and even more vigorously, Albania, have in recent years tended to defend Stalin and his role against the savage Moscow attacks.

It makes little real sense, however, to term China a Stalinist state, as it lacks the absolute personal rule and the ubiquity of terror which are regarded as the hall-marks of Stalinism. (Its ally in Europe, Albania, admittedly can be considered an embodiment of the worst aspects of Stalinism.) Nor are the domestic or foreign policies espoused by the Chinese essentially Stalinist; indeed, in their reckless and radical revolutionism they are much more akin to Trotskyism. Khrushchev himself has not been able to shake himself entirely free of Stalinism either at home or in his relations with world communism. His treatment of Albania, for example, bore many resemblances to Stalin's handling of Yugoslavia in 1948. And if the worst aspects of Stalinist rule have been modified within the Soviet Union, there are continuing features of Stalin's style, such as the treatment of artists and writers.

Among Khrushchev's closest partners in Europe, especially in East Germany, Czechoslovakia, and Rumania, the earmark of Stalinism is still more clearly evident. Only Poland and Hungary, and recently Bulgaria, have moved in step with Khrushchev in a serious programme of de-Stalinization. It would seem that in the European bloc proper, the key question, for Khrushchev, is not whether his partners carry through a significant programme of de-Stalinization, but whether they support him against the Chinese in his general line of moderation in foreign policy and the strategy of revolution.

Another confusing feature of the Sino-Soviet conflict is the habit of the contestants of describing it in terms of deviations to "left" and to "right," or as the Moscow declarations of 1956 and 1960 put it, of dangers (on the left) of dogmatism or sectarianism, and (on the right) of revisionism or reformism. These are traditional terms of differentiation and of abuse in communist disputations, and if properly understood, are useful instruments of analysis for the outside observer.

Certainly the Chinese position takes on a left wing hue, reflecting a more utopian and revolutionary spirit, and expressing itself in more uncompromising or dogmatic policies at home and abroad. Their attitude of radical discontent with the *status quo*, both social and territorial, more Trotskyist than Stalinist, no doubt appeals to the revolutionary mood of communists of Asia and other underdeveloped regions. Perhaps it also strikes a chord among some of the more ideologically minded and revolutionary Russian and East European communists, such as the Albanians and certain ousted leaders of the Bulgarian and Hungarian parties, as well as among some Western European extremist communists.

In contrast, Soviet Russia is more moderate and realist, i.e., more "rightist" in its domestic and foreign policy, and in its attitude to revolution abroad. Reflecting a mood of increasing affluence and of national territorial satisfaction, this positon has greater attraction to the more pragmatically inclined Soviet and European communist leaders, who are interested much less in the spread of revolution than in the maintenance of their own position and the steady improvement of the lot of their people and their country.

The positions of the contestants, to left and right, are not as fixed as might appear from their own use of these terms. The Chinese, for instance, shifted from a "rightist" position prior to the Hungarian revolution of 1956 to the increasingly leftist stance which they have been adopting ever since. The cleavage of Soviet and Chinese standpoints was for a time veiled by the apparent compromises reached at the Moscow conferences of 1957 and 1960, when the Chinese yielded substantially to the more moderate Soviet views on coexistence and the strategy of revolution, and both the Soviets and Chinese trained their guns on what was called "the main danger," revisionism, especially in its Yugoslav form. Even in those documents, however, "dogmatism" was also termed a threat, and one which could in certain circumstances become "the main danger."

As the Chinese position became increasingly "leftist" in the controversy with the Soviet Union, the target of Soviet propaganada became the danger to the left, although China itself was not specifically named as the culprit and Albania, in 1961, was made the chief exponent of this dread disease of "leftism" or "dogmatism." Albania, and implicitly, China, was also accused, as we have seen, of Stalinism, so that this has been increasingly identified with leftism or dogmatism, in spite of the substantial differences that exist between these two concepts. China meanwhile continued her steady drumfire of abuse of revisionism, or rightism, with Yugoslavia serving as a kind of stand-in for the real target, the Soviet Union.

More and more the Soviet Union modified the bitterness of its criticism of Yugoslav policies and sought to develop a closer and more friendly relationship between Yugoslavia and the U.S.S.R., culminating in the Tito and Khrushchev visits. Nonetheless differences remain, so that the Soviet position may perhaps best be called "centrist," with more moderate or rightist views expressed by the Yugoslav Tito, and by other influential communists such as the Italian, Togliatti. Occupying a middle position, the Soviet Union has been able to shift to either extreme, to the left at the early stage of the Sino-Soviet dispute, and now increasingly towards the right, as the chasm between China and the Soviet Union widens.

This then is the situation that exists as the Sino-Soviet conflict reaches a high pitch of intensity. The camp is riven with dissension, not only *between* parties, but *within* many parties. Leftist, rightist, and centrist tendencies exist and do not entirely coincide with Stalinist and de-Stalinizing propensities. National communism is rampant, either in the form of complete independence of action, or lesser degrees of autonomy, and in varying degrees of diversity of institutions and of standpoints.

At the moment Khrushchev has won a majority of the communist states and parties to his side, by a subtle combination of persuasion and coercion. But China and a minority of the communist movement has not been won over, and even in Europe Khrushchev has to face the defiance of little Albania. Even the most dependent and subservient of satellites, such as

Rumania, have some freedom of manoeuvre and cannot simply be forced to toe the line. Khrushchev can no longer, as Stalin once thought he was able to, snap his little finger to secure obedience. On the contrary he must deal with the international communist system, not as dictator, but as a political leader seeking to compromise differences, to persuade and to cajole, to hold the group together. This new style of politics, remarkably different to that of Stalin's day, will offer a supreme test of the political abilities of Khrushchev and his successors.

A year or two ago, most of the well-informed students of the Sino-Soviet dispute described the relationship within the world communist system as one of "divergent unity."[12] Continued divergence was anticipated, but within a framework of continuing unity. On the whole, a split between China and the Soviet Union, although not ruled out, was usually regarded as unlikely in view of the over-riding common interest of both in the maintenance of unity. Now the situation has worsened greatly, and these same observers are speaking openly of impending or actual "schism" within the communist system.[13]

In the short history of a multi-state communist system, not yet two decades old, there have already been four open breaks by individual states—Yugoslavia, Hungary, Poland, and Albania. There is no reason to doubt that there will be more such breaches in the future, and every reason to surmise that the present Sino-Soviet dispute may culminate in a complete split between China and the U.S.S.R. Both sides still profess the hope of maintaining unity, but the signs point rather in the direction of ever sharpening conflict and ultimate rupture. We may now be witnessing the twilight of the world communist system, even in its present loose form, and its dissolution into two or more separate and competing fragments.

[12] Z. Brzezinski, "The Challenge of Change in the Soviet Bloc," *Foreign Affairs*, XXXIX, No. 3 (April, 1961); R. Lowenthal, "Shifts and Rifts in the Russo-Chinese Alliance," *Problems of Communism*, VIII, No. 1 (January-February, 1959).

[13] Z. Brzezinski, "Threat or Opportunity in the Communist Schism?", *Foreign Affairs*, XLI, No. 3 (April, 1963); R. Lowenthal, "The Rise and Decline of International Communism," *Problems of Communism*, XII, No. 2 (March-April, 1963).

9

EPILOGUE: RUMANIA'S CHALLENGE
AND WESTERN RESPONSE

THE SIGNIFICANCE OF NATIONAL COMMUNISM has been amply confirmed by the events that have occurred since the writing of the articles above. The case of Rumania indeed has offered further evidence of the persistent and yet unpredictable impact of nationalism on the world communist system, and the stimulating effect of the Sino-Soviet dispute on this tendency towards greater diversity and self-determination of the separate communist nations. At the time of writing,[1] the controversy between Russia and China has reached a new pitch of intensity, suggesting that a complete split in everything except formal terms has already occurred. The two communist giants stand face to face in the world arena, abusing each other's leadership, severely criticizing the ruling party of the other, and conducting an ever mounting barrage of denunciation of every aspect of public policy of the erstwhile ally and comrade. Rumania has meanwhile taken full advantage of this conflict to stake out positions of greater and greater independence within the European communist bloc, thus accentuating all the more the multiformity of international communism, and implicitly revealing the possibilities which exist for all communist states.[2]

Rumania has become the fifth communist state in Eastern Europe to resist the Soviet Union in important spheres of action and to insist on her right to formulate her own policy and programme. Significantly, her course has been markedly

[1] August, 1964.
[2] See pp. 22, 24, 27, and the whole of Chapter 4 above on Rumania.

different from that of her predecessors in withstanding Soviet demands. Unlike Yugoslavia and Albania, she has not pursued a path which either sought, or brought about, her separation from the Soviet European bloc, although, of course, this is not excluded for the future. This was the result, not merely of Rumania's desire to remain closely associated with the Soviet Union and the bloc, but also of Soviet anxiety not to exclude her or to take actions that would have made her exit unavoidable. As a result, the defence of Rumanian rights has been accomplished quietly, for the most part in secret negotiations, and has not, at least so far, produced a full-scale political crisis of revolutionary or near-revolutionary proportions such as was occasioned by the previous resistance of Hungary and Poland. Unlike those states, too, Rumania has confined her opposition largely to external economic relations with the Soviet Union and the bloc, and has not introduced, or permitted, drastic changes in her own political system, either in leadership or in methods of government. This has not been a renewed crisis of de-Stalinization, since Rumania's policies have been implemented by her veteran Stalinist leaders themselves. There has been no challenge to the prevailing ideological position of the Soviet Union, as in the case of Yugoslavia and Albania; no serious relaxation of the control of intellectual and political life, as in the pre-crisis days in Hungary and Poland, and no drastic change in the management of industry or the conduct of agriculture, as in Poland or Yugoslavia. As in all cases of national communism, this has been a unique and distinctive one—it has been Rumanian.[3]

The major target of Rumanian opposition has been the planned economic integration of the European communist bloc,[4] and especially some of the implications drawn by the Soviet Union and other bloc members. Rumania from the

---

[3] See J. F. Brown, "Rumania Steps Out of Line," *Survey*, No. 49 (October, 1963), pp. 19–34; Randolph L. Braham, "Rumania: Onto the Separate Path," *Problems of Communism*, XIII, No. 3 (May–June, 1964), pp. 14–24; J. B. Thompson, "Rumania's Struggle with Comecon," *East Europe*, XIII, No. 6 (June, 1964), pp. 2–9.

[4] See "The Basic Principles of the International Socialist Division of Labor," *Pravda*, June 17, 1962, and the article by Khrushchev in *Kommunist*, August, 1962.

beginning accepted the underlying principles of Comecon integration, such as the "international division of labour" and the "co-ordination of economic plans," but soon began to fear that the full implementation of these principles, as envisaged by the Soviet Union and developed countries such as East Germany and Czechoslovakia, might threaten Rumania's plan of full and complete "socialist industrialization" and postpone the "levelling up" of her backward economy and the attainment of "full socialism." These worries were no doubt felt, and perhaps expressed privately, at the time of Khrushchev's visit to Rumania in the summer of 1962. It is interesting, and perhaps significant, that Khrushchev, in his concluding address in Bucharest, stressed that integration would not harm, but would help, individual countries, and indeed the small as well as the large.[5] Early in 1963, Rumania began publicly to stress the need for basing integration squarely on the principle of the equality of the member states of Comecon and respect for the right of each to determine its own plans and policies. She seems to have expressed her convictions and her concerns at successive conferences of Comecon, and to have scored something of a victory at the meeting of the executive in July, 1963. Her fears were apparently not entirely dispelled, and were occasionally revealed by strong response to views expressed in the communist bloc press which seemed to threaten her economic independence and her plans for rapid socialist industrialization.[6] Moreover, suggestions for a common plan or a single planning body for all member countries, and even for joint industrial enterprises, were firmly rejected. In the declaration of the Rumanian Central Committee of April 26, 1964, the idea of one planning body for all Comecon countries was explicitly denounced as seriously threatening "the planned management of the national economy," "one of the fundamental,

[5]*Pravda*, June 25, 1962.

[6]See, for instance, the reply to an East German journal article, to an East German book, and to a Soviet article, in *Viata Economica*, Aug. 23, 1963, June 5, and June 12, 1964, respectively. See also two important articles in the journal *Probleme Economice*, July, 1963, and September, 1963, by I. Rachmuth and M. Novac respectively, setting forth the Rumanian viewpoint.

essential, and inalienable attributes of the sovereignty of the socialist state."

The sovereignty of the socialist state requires that it effectively and fully avail itself of the means to implement practically these attributes, holding in its hands all the levers of managing economic and social life. Transmitting such levers to the competence of superstate or extrastate bodies would make of sovereignty an idea without any content.

Rejecting "exclusive solutions by some superstate authority," the statement went on:

Bearing in mind the diversity of the conditions of socialist construction, there are not and there can be no unique patterns and recipes; no one can decide what is and what is not correct for other countries or parties. It is up to every Marxist-Leninist party, it is a sovereign right of each socialist state, to elaborate, choose, or change the forms and methods of socialist construction. . . .[7]

Rumania has also not been backward in stating her independent position in the even more sensitive area of the relations of Soviet Russia and China. Indeed, the explosive conflict that has developed has not only provided her with greater freedom of manoeuvre in dealing with the Soviet Union, but has to some extent tied the hands of the latter and forced the granting of concessions. Rumania has given, it would seem, full support to the Soviet Union on the strategy of coexistence and the major political and ideological issues involved in the dispute.[8] She has, however, indicated her dissatisfaction with the methods pursued by Soviet Russia as well as by China, and through a mission to Peking in March, 1964, sought to bring the open polemic to an end and to play a mediating role. In this, her major concern has been to preserve the threatened unity of the communist movement, but at the same time to protect the independence of each of the communist states. In the April 26 declaration, the Rumanian Central Committee

[7]Partial text in *East Europe*, XIII, No. 6 (June, 1964), pp. 25–30.

[8]See, for instance, the article by the chairman of the Rumanian Council of Ministers, Ion Gheorghiu Maurer, "The Firm Foundations of the Unity of the International Communist Movement," *Problemy mira i sotsializma*, No. 11 (November, 1963), pp. 11–20.

sharply criticized the "offensive accusations" made on both sides, and in particular, the Chinese acceptance of the necessity of a split. At the same time, in a ringing statement that could be applied equally to the Soviet Union as to China, the Rumanians proclaimed:

It is the exclusive right of each party independently to work out its political line, its concrete objectives and the ways and means of attaining them, by creatively applying the general truths of Marxism-Leninism and the conclusions it arrives at from an attentive analysis of the experience of the other Communist and workers' parties.

There is not and cannot be a "parent" party and a "son" party, parties that are "superior" and parties that are "subordinate"; rather there is the great family of Communist and workers' parties which have equal rights.

No party has or can have a privileged place, or can impose its line or opinions on other parties. Each party makes its own contribution to the development of the common treasure store of Marxist-Leninist teaching, to enriching the forms and practical methods of revolutionary struggle for winning power and building socialist society.

More than once in the foregoing chapters, the difficulty, indeed the impossibility, of forecasting the future course of world communism was stressed. It was argued that national communism might appear in what seemed the most unlikely circumstances and was no longer prevented by complete Soviet control. My analysis did not predict the independent course followed by Rumania, although it did not exclude it, and in fact suggested some of the distinctive historical factors that might have occasioned it.[9] It is impossible to foresee the ultimate outcome of Rumania's actions. The mission of Maurer to Moscow, concluded on July 14, however, suggests that at least for the time being, a consensus has been achieved with the Soviet Union and that there is no likelihood of an imminent break between the two on the model of earlier cases.[10]

[9]See pp. 66–7 above.
[10]See *The New York Times*, July 15, and *Pravda*, July 15, 1964.

The classification of Eastern European communist states which was attempted above[11] retains much of its validity, although, as expected, there has been some tendency for them to shift from one category to another. In the group of states *totally independent of Soviet control*, there has been no new addition in Europe, although in Asia, China has come close to a complete breach with the Soviet Union. Albania remains almost isolated in Europe, although still retaining economic links with the other communist countries, and since March, 1963, having full diplomatic relations with Rumania. China remains her chief anchor to leeward. Yugoslavia, too, retains her cherished position of independence and non-membership in bloc organizations, although there has been a growing co-ordination of Yugoslav and Soviet foreign policies.

Rumania has preserved its full membership in the inner bloc, and her close relationship with the Soviet Union, while following a path of considerable independence, as noted above. In so doing, Rumania has clearly placed herself in the category of *semi-independent* states, along with Poland, and has extended her autonomy to crucial questions of foreign economic policy, and even intra-bloc political relations. This has been demonstrated strikingly by the return of her ambassador to Tirana, continued trade with both Albania and China, the widening of her commercial and cultural relations with the non-socialist world, and most notably, by the trade treaty concluded in 1964 with the United States. The vindication of her freedom of action in all these respects demonstrates quite conclusively the growing inability of the Soviet Union to control the actions of her one-time satellites, and suggests that the differences between the two categories of states, fully independent and semi-independent, has been greatly reduced. As in the case of Yugoslavia, the Rumanian example indicates too, the ability even of the smaller communist states to exert an appreciable influence over the course of Soviet and bloc policy.

Of the states remaining in the category of *dependent* states—

[11]See pp. 23 ff.

Bulgaria, Czechoslovakia, East Germany, and Hungary—there has been no evidence of resistance to Soviet foreign policy on the part of their leadership, nor of a substantial aspiration for autonomy or for a distinctive course in domestic affairs. They remain firm supporters of major Soviet foreign policies, including the position of the Soviet Union in the dispute with China, and have been readier than the Poles, Yugoslavs, and Rumanians, to endorse the idea of a world communist conference and a show-down with the Chinese, even at the risk of a total schism in world communism.

On matters of internal policy and institutions, dramatic changes have not occurred in any of the states, although there have been some noticeable shifts along the spectrum of differentiation in the degree of freedom. Of the "freer" states, Hungary has become somewhat *more* free, with greatly expanded travel and cultural relations with the West, and Poland distinctly *less* free, as witnessed by the protest of prominent Polish intellectuals to the government in April, complaining of restrictions on paper allocation and of censorship which threatened the development of Polish culture.[12] In Yugoslavia, too, there has been some evidence of a tightening of the reins in cultural matters, although not without publicly expressed opposition.[13] East Germany, Bulgaria, and Albania have not seriously relaxed their régime of severity. Ironically enough, Rumania herself has done little, and certainly has not embarked on a course of de-Stalinization. However, a political amnesty, substantial wage increases, extended cultural relations with the West, and a distinct tendency toward the Rumanification of names and institutions suggest that her independent course is not entirely without repercussions at home.

The extraordinary metamorphosis of Czechoslovakia, once thoroughly conformist and Stalinist, in the direction of greater freedom, bringing it somewhat closer to the Hungarian and Polish position, has been dealt with in earlier chapters. A noteworthy event in October, 1963, was the release of Arch-

[12]See *The New York Times*, April 18, 1964.
[13]*Ibid.*, June 13, 1964.

bishop Beran after twelve years' confinement. Another striking retreat by the régime was the official re-evaluation, at a Central Committee meeting in December, 1963, of the alleged danger of Slovak bourgeois nationalism, withdrawing the entire indictment of the 1950's and cancelling the expulsion from the party of Novomeský, Husák, and others.[14] A kind of stalemate, it would appear, has been reached between the régime and its critics. The position of Novotný, although undoubtedly severely shaken, has not been completely undermined, and the dissident intellectuals and journalists still find themselves under heavy fire. A full-fledged assault on the "cultural periodicals," published in the party organ, Rudé právo, on April 3, 1964, charged them with opposition to the party's line and called on the editors to adhere to party discipline and to combat expressions of "bourgeois ideology." In spite of this, and an equally tough speech by Novotný himself on April 5, at least one of the journals, the Slovak Kulturný život, failed to toe the line.[15] Meanwhile, increasingly frank and open discussion among historians, literary critics, and economists, has prompted threatening responses by official spokesmen.[16]

When the first chapter of this book was originally written (1960), the West, in my opinion, was floundering between two poles; official propaganda was making much of national communism, the differences within the bloc, and the possibility of its disintegration, whereas government policies made the bloc, as an organic whole, the target of economic and political warfare. We thus achieved the worst of both worlds. There is evidence that Western attitudes are shifting in response to the increasingly undeniable evidence of national communism. Senator J. W. Fulbright, chairman of the U.S. Foreign Rela-

[14]Published only later, Rudé právo, Feb. 29, 1964.

[15]See issue of May 1, 1964 and subsequent criticism of its defiance by the Slovak Pravda, May 15, by Novotný, Rudé právo, May 28, 1964, and by Nová mysl, No. 6, 1964. The appointing of an acting editor-in-chief, L. Mnačko, for the duration of the illness of P. Stěvček, was announced on July 4.

[16]See speech by Novotný, cited above, and by V. Koucký, Rudé právo, June 23, 1964.

tions Committee, in an important speech before the Senate, analysing the myths upon which many American foreign policies had been based, placed first in order the "master myth" that the communist bloc is a monolith, and the refusal to recognize "the great variation" in the intensity and character of the animosity of the individual members towards the West. He urged that the new "polycentrism" in world communism be understood and acted upon by Western policy.[17] George Kennan, in a significant article in *Foreign Affairs*, had already discussed the "emergence . . . of a plurality of independent or partially independent centres of political authority within the bloc," and had warned of the danger of "a lack of imagination" in the West in dealing with the problem of polycentrism.[18] Certainly many of the obstacles in the path of a reorientation of Western policy to which he then referred, remain, notably in public opinion and congressional circles of the United States.[19] The U.S. government, however, has shown an increased understanding of the new character of the communist world, and the desirability of evolving a policy that would encourage tendencies towards greater independence and greater freedom.[20] President Johnson, in an address in Lexington, Va., called for a recognition of the changes in Eastern Europe and proclaimed the American intention to "build bridges across the gulf which has divided us from Eastern Europe"—"bridges of increased trade, of ideas, of visitors, and of humanitarian aid."[21] The most notable concrete example of this policy has been the conclusion, after two weeks of negotiation in Washington, of a far-reaching agreement on trade relations between the U.S.A. and Rumania.[22]

[17]*The New York Times*, March 26, 1964.

[18]"Polycentrism and Western Policy," *Foreign Affairs*, January, 1964.

[19]A recent indication of this was the flat condemnation of "communism" without distinction, as "the enemy in every sense," and the call for liberation of all the nations of Eastern Europe from communist domination, in the platform of the Republican party adopted at its San Francisco convention. (See *The New York Times*, July 12–13, 1964.)

[20]Note the speech by the American Secretary of State, Dean Rusk, *The New York Times*, Feb. 26, 1964.

[21]*The New York Times*, May 24, 1964.

[22]*Ibid.*, June 2, 1964.

In Canada, too, there has been a shift in official policy with regard to the communist bloc from an earlier futile effort to secure a United Nations resolution for the self-determination of the nations of Eastern Europe towards a more realistic attempt to encourage economic, cultural, and other contacts with the communist countries. In an address given in Detroit on June 18, 1964, the Honourable Paul Martin, Secretary of State for External Affairs, suggested that we abandon labels no longer appropriate such as "Iron Curtain" and "satellites," and recognize that, within certain limits, the countries of Eastern Europe have "applied . . . their communism in a way which takes into account more than heretofore the differing conditions and national characteristics of the peoples concerned." Western diplomacy, he stated, had reacted intelligently to the new "opportunities for contacts and understanding, for a supple, diversified range of policies to meet each case, instead of an ineffective, precast formula to 'roll back the Iron Curtain' that increases fears behind it and therefore only serves to re-establish the Curtain in all its severity."[23] Needless to say, as a middle power, Canada is not able to exert great influence on these matters, and as an ally of the U.S.A. has been reluctant to take an initiative that would run the risk of alienating that country. Nonetheless, there are actions that Canada can take to make her presence felt in Eastern Europe and modestly to influence the course of development there and Western policy towards it. These include increased diplomatic representation in Eastern Europe, the promotion of commercial and cultural exchanges with the individual countries, and increased attention to the region in our universities and our media of mass communications.[24] A most encouraging step in this direction in early 1964 was the resumption of diplomatic relations with Hungary, and the conclusion of a three-year trade agreement.

[23]Press release, Department of External Affairs. See also his speech of Nov. 28, 1963, in the House of Commons.

[24]These were set out more fully in my chapter "Canadian Attitudes to Change and Conflict in the Soviet Bloc," in the forthcoming volume edited by E. McWhinney, *Law, Foreign Policy and the East-West Détente* (University of Toronto Press, 1964).

What of the future? Judging from the past, there is very little the West can do to determine the course of communism. Indeed, as suggested in the conclusion of the first article of this book (as originally published in *International Journal*),[25] many things are out of the control of the communist leaders, too. The elemental shifts and explosions within the communist world in the past decade were not caused by Western policy, or even foreseen by Western scholarship or intelligence. There was little that we could have done to promote or even to influence the events in Yugoslavia, Poland, and Hungary. It was equally unlikely that we could anticipate, or promote, changes, then undiscernible, in, say, Czechoslovakia or Bulgaria. The "little" we could do was to avoid two extremes in our thinking and our acting concerning Eastern Europe and the communist bloc.

The one extreme was to assume that communism was inevitably one and indivisible, to be treated accordingly as a single enemy bloc, and to be attacked in a uniform fashion by our economic policy, our diplomacy, and our propaganda. Such an attitude, manifested, for instance, in begrudging aid to Poland and Yugoslavia, or in trade embargoes on all communist countries, or shrill propaganda against the evil of communism, could only drive the members of the bloc closer and closer and push all of them into more and more radical policies. If there were continuing differences of opinion within the leadership, especially in Russia or China, this attitude on the part of the West could only encourage the victory of the groups or persons advocating strict unity of the bloc. The opinion expressed by Christian Herter, then U.S. Secretary of State, concerning Moscow's responsibility for the actions of the entire bloc, moved in this same unfruitful direction.[26]

The other extreme to be avoided was to seek openly to divide and separate the communist states from each other, to

[25]The final paragraphs of the original article are here reproduced without essential change.

[26]Herter was reported as saying that "the demand for recognition as the leader of the Communist world places upon the Russians a degree of responsibility for the actions of other members of the bloc that is very real" (*The New York Times*, Oct. 7, 1959).

pit one or other against Moscow, and to break up the bloc as a whole. Crude policies seeking to exploit national communism to our own advantage, such as open calls for resistance to Soviet communism, or to communism itself, were likely to boomerang, forcing the satellites to be more careful in their assertion of independence, and driving Russia or China to reprisals to defend the unity of the bloc, thus bringing the world to the brink of war arising out of local rebellions.

Our guiding assumption should be, I then argued, that the most likely trend of events will be an evolution *within* communism, rather than its total *replacement by* another system. With this in mind, our attitude towards communism should be subtle and restrained, avoiding loud propaganda and threats of intervention, and encouraging the peaceful evolution of national communism within the communist bloc. All our actions should be measured against the tests that they do not discourage the emergence of trends towards national communism or of leaders favourable to this view, that they do not stimulate the rise of radical spokesmen of bloc unity and uniformity, and that they do not encourage extremes of national communism leading to revolt and civil war, and Soviet military intervention. Such policies of moderation can be found in the expansion of foreign trade with communist countries, the offering of aid to some or all of them, and the widest possible cultural exchange with the communist world. All this must be done in a mood of modesty as to our own ability to affect the outcome decisively, and in a spirit of humility as to the inscrutability of the ultimate outcome of the forces operating within the communist world.

INDEX